ŁASTERN
PROVENCE
Côte d'Azur to the Alps

a countryside guide

John and Pat Underwood

SUNFLOWER BOOKS

First published 2002
by Sunflower Books™
12 Kendrick Mews
London SW7 3HG, UK

ISBN 1-85691-191-8

Important note to the reader

We have tried to ensure that the descriptions and maps in this book are error-free at press date. The book will be updated, where necessary, whenever future printings permit. It will be very helpful for us to receive your comments (sent in care of the publishers, please) for the updating of future printings.

   We also rely on those who use this book — especially walkers — to take along a good supply of common sense when they explore. Conditions can change fairly rapidly, and *storm damage or bulldozing may make a route unsafe at any time*. If the route is not as we outline it here, and your way ahead is not secure, return to the point of departure. *Never attempt to complete a tour or walk under hazardous conditions!* Please read carefully the Country code on page 8 and the notes on pages 61-63, as well as the introductory comments at the beginning of each tour and walk (regarding road conditions, equipment, grade, distances and time, etc). Explore *safely*, while at the same time respecting the beauty of the countryside.

Cover photograph: Notre-Dame-de-Gratemoine, on the Route Napoléon below Séranon (Car tour 4 and Walk 22)
Page 1: old post office at Séranon (Car tour 4)
Above: goats lolling about the Gorge de Guègues belvedere on the Route des Crêtes in the Grand Canyon du Verdon (Car tour 8)

Photographs: John Underwood
Maps: John Underwood
A CIP catalogue record for this book is available from the British Library.
Printed and bound in the UK by Brightsea Press, Exeter

10 9 8 7 6 5 4 3 2 1

✿ Contents

4   Landscapes of eastern Provence

Vineyards below the Montagne Ste-Victoire (Car tour 10). The perfect harmony between man and nature is the secret of the French countryside.

Preface

This two-volume *Landscapes of Provence* will plunge you into
the most beautiful countryside between the Alps and the
Pyrenees. Nature has prepared the canvas for these landscapes
over millions of years, but man has added colour, form and
texture. The straight bold strokes of lavender, vineyards,
planes and poplars streak across plateaus; bridges and aque-
ducts arc gracefully over rivers; sturdy stone towers with
whimsical wrought-iron bell-cages stipple the hilltops.

If the harmony between man and nature is the key to the
beauty of this countryside, nowhere is it better conveyed than
in the paintings of the Impressionists and Post-Impressionists
so intimately associated with the south of France — Cézanne,
Van Gogh, Monet. Almost everywhere you travel a master-
piece comes to life — an isolated farmhouse awash in fields
of scarlet poppies, the limestone ribs of Ste-Victoire rising
above a bib of emerald vineyards, stars burning out in a cobalt
blue sky over the lamplit lanes of Arles.

This is a guide to the outdoors, written for those who prize
the countryside as highly as a cathedral. We want to take you
along the most beautiful roads by car and, when the opportunity presents itself, park, don walking boots, pick up the
rucksack and *participate* in this landscape. France caters mar-
vellously for all grades of walkers, but *precise* descriptions of
tours and walks for motorists are rare. Most touring guides

concentrate on history and architecture, while books for walkers outline the famous long-distance routes (the Grandes Randonnées). But these 'GR' footpaths are sometimes very demanding and, being linear, are in any case unsuitable for motorists.

Our aim has been to describe **car tours** running from the Italian border to the Pyrenees through *many* (certainly not all!) of the most beautiful landscapes in the south of France. The **walks** chosen — from a vast network of possible routes — are those we feel offer the greatest sense of satisfaction for the effort involved, taking into account the high temperatures and humidity during much of the year. Most of the routes are circular.

This first volume of *Landscapes of Provence* travels from the Riviera to the Alps and as far west as Aix-en-Provence, from where the second book will take you to the foothills of the Pyrenees. Use *Landscapes of the Pyrenees* to carry on to the Atlantic coast!

Bibliography

It must be stressed that this is a *countryside* guide, meant to be used in conjunction with a standard guide or guides covering the area. We find the Michelin guides indispensable, and always take along the following:

Michelin Red Guide: *always travel with the **latest** edition.* Not only is it useful for finding accommodation (and telephoning ahead), but the excellent town plans are *essential* for finding your way round the cities.

Michelin Green Guides: French Riviera (available in English), **Alpes du Sud** (in French only), **Provence** (available in English).

Of the plethora of standard guides on the market, the **Cadogan Guide to the South of France** matches most closely the territory covered in the two volumes of *Landscapes of Provence;* its presentation and suggestions for places to stay should appeal to 'Landscapers'.

Many French **walking guides** are now available locally. Few tourist offices hand out free walk descriptions (as they did in the past); they

Car tour 7: The Cadières de Brandis (top right) rise above the turquoise-to-jade Verdon near the Clue de Chasteuil. A misty morning like this, early in October, is a sure sign that a perfect day lies ahead!

prefer to sell you a book or map. If they *do* offer a free handout, it is likely to be virtually useless (as we found at Les Baux). The only exceptions *(at time of writing)* are the free pamphlets from the St-Cézaire tourist office and two beautifully-produced guides from the Conseil Général des Alpes-Maritimes: *Randos Moyen Pays* and *Randos Haut Pays*. Ask for these at any tourist office in Alpes-Maritimes while stocks last! We doubt that this munificence will survive much longer.

Note that most French publications tend to describe walks *very briefly:* make sure that you can form a mental picture of the walk in advance — the climb, the distance, the terrain. Read carefully what we say on page 62 under 'Waymarking, grading, safety'.

MAPS
At the top of each **car tour** we refer to the appropriate **Michelin maps** (yellow series; scale 1:200,000). For this book you will need maps 81 and 84 *or* the *larger-format* map 245 (Provence/Côte d'Azur); you may

like to supplement these with *larger-scale* (1:100,000) maps 114 (French Riviera/Var/Verdon Gorges) and 115 (Côte d'Azur/Alpes-Maritimes).

For **walking** we hope that you will find the maps in the book sufficient. But if you plan to do a lot of walking in a given area, *do* buy the relevant **IGN 'Top 25' map**. These maps (scale 1:25,000), published by the Institut Géographique National (the French 'OS'), are widely available in shops, petrol stations and kiosks locally, or they may be purchased before you travel from your usual map supplier. For each walk in this book, the corresponding IGN map number is shown.

Two other useful maps were available at nominal charge at time of writing:
Tourist map of the Esterel, scale 1:25,000, published by the Office National des Forêts (tourist office in St-Raphaël or Fréjus);
Ste-Victoire et Secteur Zola, scale 1:25,000, published by the Association des Excursionnistes Provençaux (tourist office in Aix).

☀ Picnicking

Picnicking possibilities are limitless in Provence — especially if you follow the example of the locals and tour with a collapsible table and chairs (available at very low cost in supermarkets). Picnic areas with tables are encountered on some of the tours; these are indicated in the touring notes and on the touring map with the symbol ⊼. All the walks in the book offer superb picnic settings, but on days when you are planning *only* to tour by car it is helpful to have some idea of where you might stop for an alfresco lunch. At the top of each car tour we suggest a few picnic spots, favourites of ours over the years. They are highlighted on the touring map, with a **P** printed in green. Where possible we have chosen places where there is something firm and dry to sit on.

A country code for walkers and motorists

Bear in mind that all land in Provence is privately owned, whether by an individual or a district. All waymarked walks and other routes described in this book are permissive, *not* 'rights of way'. Behave responsibly, never forgetting the danger of forest fires.

- **Do not light fires** except at purpose-built barbecues. *Never park blocking a fire-fighting track!*
- **Do not frighten animals**. When driving, always stop the car until the livestock have moved off the road.
- **Walk quietly** through all farms, hamlets and villages, **leaving any gates just as you find them**.
- **Protect all wild and cultivated plants**. Don't pick wild flowers or uproot saplings. Obviously crops are someone's livelihood and should not be touched. **Never walk over cultivated land!**
- **Take all your litter away with you**.
- **Stay on the path**. Don't take short cuts on zigzag paths; this damages vegetation and hastens erosion, eventually destroying the main path.

✴ Touring

The ten car tours in this first volume of *Landscapes of Provence* take you north from Nice to the Alps and then west to Aix-en-Provence. While a few important centres have been omitted for lack of space, we feel that the two books present a comprehensive overview of the most beautiful landscapes. And as a change from motoring, we highly recommend the delightful train journey described on pages 130-131.

The touring notes are brief: they include little history or information readily available in other publications (see Bibliography, page 6). *We concentrate instead on route planning:* each tour has been devised to follow **the most beautiful roads** in the relevant region and to take you to the starting point of some delightful **walks**. (Further information about some of the places visited can be found in the notes for the walks.)

The large fold-out map is designed to give you a quick overview of the touring routes, walks and picnic places *in both volumes*. At the start of each tour we refer to the relevant Michelin touring map(s), which are so handy to use in

Madone de Fenestre, with snow-capped Mt Gélas (Car tour 2)

conjunction with their *Red Guide*. **Important:** Both driver and navigator should look over the **latest Michelin Red Guide before** entering or leaving any large city, so that you have some idea of where you are heading and the landmarks en route. It is *never* as simple as it looks on the touring maps, and *hours* can be wasted twirling in spaghetti loops on ring roads round cities like Aix!

The **touring bases** are, obviously, just *suggestions*, and the tours can be joined at any point en route (the major villages are shown at the top of each tour). Since some of the territory covered is well away from popular tourist areas, we chose bases which offered not only hotels, but *our* essential requirements for making an early-morning start: a petrol station and a mini-market!

Because this is a *countryside* guide, the tours often bypass the villages en route, however beautiful or historically important. We do, however, use symbols to alert you to the cultural highlights (a **key to the symbols** used is on the touring map).

Some other points to keep in mind: **petrol stations** are often closed on Sundays and holidays in the remote areas covered by some of the tours. **Cyclists** do *not* travel in single file, nor is cycling confined to weekends. But on Sundays some roads will be closed off for cycle races: you will have to take a short *déviation*. *Déviations*, however, may *not* be short when they involve roadworks. Especially in spring, long stretches of road will be closed, and you may have to go up to 50km out of your way! French **arrow signposting** can be mystifying until you get used to it. Finally, remember that **Sundays and holidays** are a nightmare at the most popular 'sights', and places like the Grand Canyon du Verdon and Madone d'Utelle should be avoided. Our tours have been planned not only to take you on the most beautiful roads, but to reach the three-star attractions before or after the crowds. If you follow our advice, but you *still* encounter crowds, we have to admit: we never visit Provence in July or August.

Tour 1: THE CORNICHE D'OR AND THE ESTEREL

Nice • Antibes • Cannes • Massif de l'Esterel • Nice

174km/108mi; 5-6h driving; Michelin map 84, or larger scale map 115. (The Forestry Department map of the Esterel referred to in the Bibliography on page 7 is also useful for both touring and walking.)
Walks en route: 5-7, also many other walk combinations in the Esterel (see text below and map pages 74-75); Walks 1-4 and 8-10 are easily reached from Nice. *This tour assumes an early morning start, so that the red rock of the Esterel can be seen at its best with a low sun rising in the east (and so that* the busy coastal roads will be less crowded). *Be sure to fill up with petrol before turning into the Esterel, and have your picnic with you. The short road to Mont Vinaigre is narrow and not built up at the side.*
Picnic suggestions: There are good picnic places *all over* the **Esterel**, but particularly pleasant settings are the lake near the Grenouillet ford (just as you start into the massif; rocks to sit on and some shade) or the dam 30 minutes along Walk 5 (photographs page 73).

This tour skirts our favourite stretch of coast in the south of France; it wins — by a nose — over the Riviera proper (Nice to Menton, Tour 2). This may be because it is less built up, but what stays in the memory are the turquoise-to-jade creeks (*calanques*) below the road, pierced by blades of crimson rock. Beyond Cap d'Antibes, we come upon the glorious sweep of the Golfe de la Napoule and then follow the Golden Corniche above these *calanques*. Heading inland, we climb into the 'rock garden' of the Esterel, where spring-flowering *maquis* and lime-green pines shimmer against yet more fiery-red porphyry rock.

Leave **Nice** *on the N98 (coastal road to* ANTIBES*), then follow signs for* CAP D'ANTIBES.

One could easily spend half a day at **Antibes★** (15km *i✝■M*); save Antibes and other towns along the coast for another day, when you could easily visit by public transport and not have the hassle of finding a parking space.
You round the small peninsula of **Cap d'Antibes★**, with its luxury hotels, immaculate gardens and fine coastal views (☎). This road rejoins the coastal N98 at **Juan-les-Pins** (*i*). After rounding the **Pointe de la Croisette** (☎) you come to **Cannes★** (33km *i✝■M*) and the beautiful sweep of the **Golfe de Napoule**. Save at least a day for your visit to Cannes. Beyond **La Napoule** (*i■M*), now following the **Corniche d'Or**

(Golden Corniche), you skim past one resort after another.
Walk 6 begins and ends at **Théoule-sur-Mer** (■), coming back into the village via the viewpoint at the **Pointe de l'Aiguille** (☎). The modern honeycombe of **Port-la-Galère** snuggles into terraces bordering the bay. It is worth stopping at the **Pointe de l'Esquillon★** (☎) for the fine views of the coast all the way back east to Cap d'Antibes. The red porphyry cliffs of the Esterel rise up to the right.
You pass **Miramar** and then **Le Trayas**, a strung-out settlement on wooded slopes beside the sea. Now the sharply-indented *calanques* create a breathtaking landscape down to your left. Just beyond the **Pointe du Cap Roux** there is an especially fine

11

Left: coastal view towards the Golfe de Napoule, from the Sentier des Balcons de la Côte d'Azur. Above: the red porphyry rock of Cap Roux (top); boars near the Roussiveau Forestry house. See also photographs on page 73.

viewpoint (📷) over this setting at the **Pointe de l'Observatoire★**. Beyond **Anthéor**, at **Agay** (64km *i*), we leave the coast to delve into the **Esterel Massif★**.

Turn right on the D100 for VALESCURE* and, 1.5km uphill, fork right on a narrow tarmac road (which may only be signposted to PIC DE L'OURS after you have turned).

Cap Roux dominates the landscape on the right, as you pass to the left of the **Maison Forestière du Gratadis**.

At the junction, go right for PIC DE L'OURS (perhaps refer now to the large-scale map on pages 74-75).

*You ford the **Grenouillet** stream; a lovely lake is on the left here.*

At the next junction (Carrefour de Mourrefrey), keep straight ahead, where the Cap Roux road comes in from the right (signposted to the Rocher de St-Barthélemy).

Cap Roux rises brilliantly above you here. Travelling on the north side of St-Pilon and Cap Roux,

you come to the **Site de la Ste-Baume**, from where footpaths lead up to a cave-chapel dedicated to St-Honorat (waymarked with a chapel 'symbol'; 1h return) and a viewing table on the summit of Cap Roux (2h circuit; 'rocks' symbol). The paths are shown on the map on pages 74-75, but *beware:* they are quite strenuous, vertiginous in places, and not recommended on windy days. There are fine views to the sea as you climb through an extraordinary landscape of rounded red rock hills freckled with *maquis*. At the **Col de l'Evêque** you head right into a one-way system, continuing round the Pic d'Aurelle to the **Col des Lentisques** (footpath to the summit of Pic d'Aurelle; 📷 45min return).

Turn right at the col.

Splendid coastal views unravel as you climb, and there are ample opportunities to park. Red rock falls away straight below you, and you look out over the Corniche d'Or all the way back to Cap d'Antibes. Le Trayas is framed by the tip of Point Esquillon, and the

---

But for Walk 7, continue for 2km to the monument at **Cap du Dramont, where you can park.*

Nice is a superb base from which to explore eastern Provence. Apart from the setting (photograph page 65), there are frequent festivals (above), markets galore, and some superb architecture (including curiosities like the Russian church shown left). Best of all, many walks are easily reached by public transport. What better way to spend a winter's weekend?

Lérin Islands shimmer in the mirror of Napoule Bay.

At the **Col Notre-Dame** (76.5km), a track off to the right leads to the summits of the Petites and Grosses Grues (☞ 1h30min return). You could also climb to Pic de l'Ours (☞ 1h30min return); these routes are shown on the map on pages 74-75.

The main tour turns back south from this pass*; keep right, into the one-way system at the **Col des Lentisques**. Once back at the **Col de l'Evêque**, turn right, again on a two-way road. Just under 4km along fork right for MAISON DU GRAIADIS, AGAY.

After passing the lake again and crossing the ford, turn right for PERTHUS and MAL INFERNET.

*But from the Col Notre-Dame one can continue for another 5km to the Col des Trois Termes. After about 2.5km, at the **Col de la Cadière**, the GR51 can be followed northeast along the **Sentier des Balcons de la Côte d'Azur**. It is worth walking along this level track for 2km/30min, to the Rocher des Monges, just past the junction for the Col de Théoule. Beyond the Col de la Cadière the road deteriorates and is closed to motor vehicles beyond the Col des Trois Termes, so you cannot drive through to the N7.

Some 400m along, at the **Col de Belle-Barbe**, pull up to park for Walk 5. Or continue straight on for PERTHUS. The twin summits of **Perthus** rise ahead on the right. While none of the peaks in the Esterel is very high, the deep ravines, jagged crags and tortuous roads all conspire to convey that enjoyable feeling of being 'in the mountains'.

When you come to the **Col du Mistral** (*beyond which the road is closed to motor vehicles*), retrace your route via the Col de Belle-Barbe and, at the lake, keep straight ahead, to continue past the Maison Forestière du Gratadis.

At the D100, turn right for VALESCURE/ST-RAPHAEL. Take a km reading here, as your next turn-off is not very obvious. You will follow this road for 6.5km.

Passing small scattered vineyards and new housing developments, keep straight on towards Valescure at the roundabouts. Soon you come into the beautiful **Valescure** golfing development, studded with graceful parasol pines.

After 6.5km along the D100, where a left turn leads to St-Raphaël, turn right on the inconspicuously-signposted Route Forestière de la Louve (closed from 9pm to 6am).

There is a dramatic view to Mont Vinaigre from here.

13

*At the **Carrefour de la Colle Douce** fork left for LES ADRETS/N7. Cross the Pont de la Bécasse and take the second right for MONT VINAIGRE.*

Now you have joined the ancient **Via Aurelia** which once linked Rome with Arles via Genoa, St-Raphaël, Fréjus and Aix. Some 3m/9ft wide, it was paved and cambered; as it approached the various staging posts, pavements were raised along the side for pedestrians. Long after Roman times this remained the only road to Italy; today the N7 follows much the same route east of Mont Vinaigre. You pass the **Maison Forestière des Cantonniers** on the left — a fit subject for a Utrillo canvas, with its turquoise shutters. Some 1.5km further on you come to the **Maison Forestière du Malpey**. Looking at this pretty rose-hued building in idyllic surroundings, it's hard to conjure up the past … the 18th century, when this stretch of the Aurelian Way was the most dangerous spot on the infamous 'Esterel road' and menaced by brigands. Gaspard de Besse (who met an especially grisly death at the age of 25) was the most famous among them; his hideout was a cave in the side of nearby Mont Vinaigre.

At the fork here bear right for MONT VINAIGRE. At the next fork (0.6km) head left (where a track goes right to Plan de l'Esterel and the Aire de l'Olivier). The narrow road is somewhat vertiginous.

There is a typically complex relay station at the parking area and another on the summit of **Mont Vinaigre★** (618m/2027ft; 109km), the highest point in the massif and a 200m walk away. From the old watchtower there is a splendid panorama; in the south and east you can trace all of the day's tour.

From Vinaigre return to the Malpey forestry house and turn right. Turn right again at the N7 (113km).

The Auberge des Adrets at the **Carrefour du Logis-de-Paris** (3km along) was one of de Besse's favourite watering holes.

*Continue on the N7 for 17km, until you can join the motorway back to **Nice** (174km).*

Tour 2: THE RIVIERA AND THE MERCANTOUR

Nice • Menton • Sospel • Col de Turini • La Bollène-Vésubie • St-Martin-Vésubie • Le Boréon • Madone de Fenestre • Vallon de la Gordolasque • St-Martin-Vésubie

216km/134mi; about 12h driving over two days; Michelin map 84 or 245, or larger-scale map 115. For day two of the tour (especially if you plan to walk), it is very helpful to have IGN map 3741 OT, which you can buy in St-Martin-Vésubie.

Walks en route: 8, 9, (10), 11-16; Walks 1-4 are easily reached direct from Nice.

St-Martin-Vésubie, halfway through this tour (109km), makes a convenient overnight base. Driving will be very slow throughout; almost all the roads are winding. We use three main access roads into the Mercantour National Park: the valleys of Le Boréon, Madone de Fenestre and the Gordolasque. If you wish to visit one of the valleys on the first day of the tour, choose Le Boréon: it is the shortest, easiest road. All the roads are good and amply wide, except in the valley of the Gordolasque, where the road is very narrow and not always built up at the side (conversely, in some places it is very tightly hemmed in by stone walls). Avoid this road on Sundays

and holidays, when it will be quite busy; passing can be a nightmare. There are no petrol stations between Sospel and St-Martin (50km) or during the whole of day two in the Mercantour (107km). Note that some roads will be closed from October to May, due to snow or rock-falls. Note also, if you plan to walk, that as late as June snow may still be lying on the paths we describe; it's a wise precaution to check at the National Park office in St-Martin, to make sure that you won't need crampons. The refuges should be open on weekends from April until 15 June, and daily thereafter until 15 September. Do not rely on this; always carry your own provisions!

Picnic suggestions: The chapel steps of **Notre-Dame-de-la-Menour** north of Sospel make a fine perch above the Gorges du Paion. Almost anywhere during the circuit of the **Authion** mountain (optional detour; see box and photograph page 21) you will find grassy slopes or old ruins to sit on (be sure to park in a lay-by on this narrow road). On day two of the tour, **Le Boréon** itself is a lovely setting, by the lake or falls, but why not follow Walk 13 to the **Chalet Vidron** (30min), to picnic under fruiting rowans in autumn or to seek out gentians in spring? At **Madone de Fenestre** the grassy slopes near the cross (photograph pages 8-9) give you a superb outlook to the *cirque* or, if you start out on Walk 14, you can picnic overlooking the stream (photograph page 90, bottom). The Gordolasque torrent near the **Pont du Countet** is incredibly beautiful, with the outlook shown on pages 91 and 92.

Sospel, on the banks of the Bévéra

15

Perhaps more than any other tour in this book, this one sums up why we have all come to France ... and why the French hardly ever feel the need to travel anywhere else. First we follow the Grande Corniche above the coast from Nice to Menton, above the fabulous settings of Monaco and Monte Carlo. How many films this conjures up in the mind's eye! How many triumphant roles — and tragedies — have been played out in real life against this backdrop! From the Riviera we quickly climb into the Turini Forest and magnificent firs that would feel at home in Finland. Finally we're in the heart of the southern Alps. Chalets dot the landscape, cow bells ring out, lush green pastureland lies below snow-capped peaks ... a Swiss calendar landscape. What surprises most is that we seem to have moved almost effortlessly through three different *countries* in not much over an hour's driving from the coast. Why indeed would the French go anywhere else?

*Leave **Nice** by heading east along the Promenade des Anglais; follow GRANDE CORNICHE, LA TURBIE. (D2564).*

You quickly climb to the **Grande Corniche★**, originally built by Napoleon along the ancient Via Julia Augusta, the route the Romans first laid down during their campaigns to conquer the Maritime Alps. This magnificent road offers far-reaching views all the way along. Stop first at the **Belvédère d'Eze★** (11km 📷), from where you look up to the Alps, back to Cap Ferrat and ahead — over the three Corniche roads — to cliffs plunging into the sea. From the **Col d'Eze** (📷) 1km further on, there is a brilliant view focussing on the church and château in Eze, perched on a rocky spike above the sea. This is one of most photographed landscapes in France. Some 2km along there is an even finer view back over Eze, with Cap Ferrat, the airport and Cap d'Antibes behind it.

Beyond a road down to Eze, La Turbie suddenly appears ahead: the blinding-white **Trophée des Alpes★** rises behind a church with a cupola of glazed tiles. **La Turbie** (18km 🏛M📷) developed around this fascinating monument. Built in 6BC from almost pure-white local stone, it originally rose to 50m/165ft. It stood on the Via Julia Augusta, in commemoration of Roman victories over 44 different Alpine tribes. Sacked at the end of the Roman Empire, the trophy was mined by the troops of Louis XIV and then used as a quarry (the church incorporates some of its stone); a museum relates its skilful restoration in the early 1900s. Walk 8 begins at La Turbie — a magnificent hike that descends through Eze to the coast. From La Turbie the road continues below the Monte Carlo radio transmitter on conical Mont Agel.

Head right for MENTON where the D53 goes left to Peille (Walk 3), then go left for ROQUEBRUNE, MENTON (where the D53 goes right to Beausoleil and Monaco).

Now Cap Martin (Walk 10) is seen ahead. Pull over to the right in front of the Vista Palace Hotel at the **Belvédère du Vistaëro★** (23km 📷), with more fine views to the Italian coast and down over Monaco, with the **Tête de Chien** (photograph page 71) rising above it.

Monaco from the Jardin Exotique (above); Gorges de la Vésubie (right)

Curve left in front of the hotel (but then keep right for ROQUEBRUNE, where a left turn goes up to the motorway).

You descend looking ahead to the ancient hill village of Roquebrune. Just 1km after entering **Roquebrune-Cap-Martin★** (24km *i*▮), turn left uphill into the centre. The village has managed to preserve much of its medieval character. The 10th-century fortress, with its castle keep, was erected as a defence against Saracen raids. If you are one step ahead of the coaches, wander through the narrow stepped and covered passageways, with their medieval houses, and soak up the atmosphere which so appealed to Sir Winston Churchill. Walk 10 could begin here.

When you join the N7 below Roquebrune, turn left for MENTON.

You pass above **Cap Martin★** (Walk 10, photograph page 81) and come into **Menton★** (31km *i*♣M), sheltered below a backdrop of mountains. At the first opportunity, turn right, to the seafront, then turn left. There is a pleasant view of the old town as you sweep along the seafront. Park near the 17th-century fort housing the Cocteau Museum (on your right, where the road swings left), if you plan a *quick* visit to the town. Climb up towards the Italianate campanile, where you will come into a delightful square overlooking the coast, the Parvis St-Michel. Two churches open onto this square: the splendid 15/18th-century baroque church of St-Michel and the 17/19th-century Chapel of the White Penitents. More steps will take you up into Rue du Vieux-Château and to the cemetery, from where there is an even finer view over the old town and port. Resolve to return and spend a day here, to see all the museums and gardens. And to do Walk 9, which uses very convenient buses from Menton.

Leave Menton on the D2566 for SOSPEL.

Soon you pass under a very impressive motorway bridge arcing over the valley, through which high mountains are seen ahead. Start climbing in hairpins up the industrialised **Carei Valley**. From **Monti** (halfway along the route of Walk 9) there is a pleasant view across the valley to Castellar (where Walk 9 ends), on a promontory. Beyond a turn-off to Castellar, you begin to climb in hairpins (⊼) through the **Forêt de Menton**. The semi-circular **Viaduc du Caramel** is seen on the other side of the valley, and soon you curve past this old railway bridge, built in the 1920s (see page 130).

Keep right at a Y-fork (⊼) for SOSPEL PAR LE COL DE CASTILLON.

You pass below **Castillon**, an artists' colony, where the church has a beautiful glazed-tile cupola and much trompe l'œil decoration is in evidence. An impressive, deeply-wooded valley is on your left on the climb to the **Col de Castillon**, where you go through a short tunnel.

Beyond the tunnel, turn right on the D2566 for SOSPEL.

Enticing views of the mountains ahead (📷) and olive groves in the immediate vicinity accompany you on the spectacular hairpin descent into **Sospel** (49km *i*⛪; Walk 11), where the Renaissance façade and beautiful 10/11th-century Romanesque bell-tower of the classical church (the largest in Alpes-Maritimes) rise high above the surrounding rooftops. Park by the river. Cross the 11th-century bridge shown on pages 14-15; its toll- or watch-tower, which was destroyed in World War II, has been rebuilt and now houses the excellent tourist office. Go ahead to the ancient fountain in the Place St-Nicholas (photograph page 83), then cross back over the bridge and walk to the church square on the right bank, with its beautifully-decorated trompe l'œil buildings.

Leave Sospel on the D2566 for COL DE TURINI, MOULINET.

Now you're really *in* the mountains, and the magnificent Authion rises up ahead. Cross the river **Guiou** in a lovely setting of planes and climb the **Bévéra Valley**, passing a waterfall on the right. Soon you're in the **Gorges du Piaon★**, where striated honey-coloured cliffs hang out above you. The road ahead loops ever upwards on stone-built terraces, a 'Great Wall of China' curling lovingly round each limb of the landscape. Watch for the chapel of **Notre-Dame-de-la-Menour** on the right, and park just below it. Don't try to climb to the chapel from here; walk ahead along the road, then steps *on the left* will take you over the pedestrian footbridge to this tiny chapel with its Renaissance façade (⛪). Nearby are fine views down to the emerald-green river. **Moulinet** (70km) is a pretty village in a verdant basin; its church is also stylishly dressed in fashionable trompe l'œil.

Nothing quite prepares you for the splendour of the **Turini Forest★**, an enormous mixed woodland blanketing the heights

La Bollène rising above the Vésubie Valley, with the mountains of the Mercantour to the north

between the Bévéra and Vésubie valleys. Climbing at first through a great variety of deciduous trees with sprinklings of sea pines, you quickly come into the 'real' forest, dominated by larch and magnificent pines. The best time to be here is in autumn, when the delicate red and gold tracery of the deciduous trees is a perfect foil for the towering dark firs — some as much as 50m/150ft high. Bright red berries, thick as cherry clusters, weigh down the rowans.

Four roads converge at the **Col de Turini** (74km ▲*✕), where Walk 12 begins and ends. It's also one of our favourite places to take a break or stay overnight.

Bear right at the col, then go left on the D70 for LA BOLLENE-VESUBIE. (Or keep straight ahead here on the D68, to make a 17km circuit of the Authion★; see box overleaf.)

The D70 descends the valley of the Bollène in hairpins, still buttressed by a 'Great Wall of China'. Not far beyond a tunnel, pull over left at the chapel of **St-Honorat** (*✝⌕ 戸). From the terrace you enjoy the lovely view shown opposite. The road descends through chestnut trees, bypassing the centre of **La Bollène-Vésubie** (94km *✝戸), a small hilltop village of 18th-century houses clustered round the church.

Below La Bollène, turn right on the D2565 for ST-MARTIN-VESUBIE.

Beyond a turn-off left to the *new* village of Roquebillière, look up right to Belvédère, attractively strung out along a ridge. Just after this view, you pass the road to Belvédère and the Gordolasque Valley (the 66km-point in day two of the tour, a *very* sharp right turn from this approach). Now Mt Tournairet rises on the other side of the teal-blue **Vésubie River**. You pass below the old part of **Roquebillière**, where the

Romanesque church tower has a glazed tile cupola. What strikes the eye immediately is the colour of the stone in this area — brown-to-beige, but strongly streaked with mauve, burgundy and sienna. Soon you may notice picnic areas on both sides of the road (no tables) bearing a sign, *pacages interdits* — 'no grazing'. This is because the traditional *transhumance* (see page 133) is once again taking place in many parts of the country. Beyond a hydro-electric power station down left, you pass through **Les Châtaig-niers** (戸). Even though some new houses have been built, this picture-postcard old hamlet (named for the red-flowering chestnut trees fronting the older houses) is still exquisite.

As you enter **St-Martin-Vésubie** (109km *i✝⌕), at the confluence of Boréon and Madone de Fenestre valleys, the road makes a tight U-turn in front of the tourist office (just where the bulbous tower of the Chapel of the White Penitents rises ahead). Park immediately beyond this turn and walk to the tourist office; the office of the Mercantour National Park (with a small library) is diagonally opposite. Both merit a visit before you explore the town, a good place to shop for books and maps, picnics and walking gear. The 12th-century statue of Our Lady of Fenestre is on view in the 17th-century church between October and June; in summer she resides at the chapel visited on day two of the tour.

On the second day of the tour, leave St-Martin (0km) heading north on the main D2565 (the direction you were heading when you rounded the tight U-turn).

If you haven't already done so, *fill up* with petrol now (⛽).

Just over 2km past the petrol

station, turn right on the D89 for
LE BOREON, *then turn left almost
immediately.*

It seems as if you have crossed the
border into Switzerland: alpine
chalets dot lush green pastures.
You're following a 15th-century
salt route: salt from the pans at
Hyères was taken by mule via
Nice, Utelle and St-Martin up this
valley and over the mountains into
Italy.
Having crossed the Boréon stream
at Les Trois Ponts (the Italian
border until 1947), you reach **Le
Boréon★** (8.5km 🏔🍴), at the
entrance to the **Mercantour
National Park**. There's a lovely
waterfall and small lake here.
Continue ahead through this fairy-
tale setting.

*At a T-junction, turn right on the
D189 (🍴), for the VACHERIE DU
BOREON.*

The road narrows, but is still
comfortably wide. The tar ends at
a parking area (11.5km 🍴).

*To park for Walk 13, continue
ahead here on a rough track for
another 1km, following PARKING
SUPERIEUR DU BOREON.*

From the *vacherie* return towards
St-Martin.

*At a roundabout just before
joining the main road, turn left for
MADONE DE FENESTRE. At the next
junction, 1.5km along, bear left on
the D94.*

As you climb this valley, with the
stream on your right, magnificent
pines sweep down from the
summits of Piagu on the left and
Palu on the right. They form a V,
and you head straight for craggy
Mont Ponset, best seen when
capped with snow. Some 6km
uphill you pass a huge pipe crossing the river at **Les Pontets**; it
carries water from the lake at Le
Boréon all the way to the power
station near Les Châtaigniers. The

burbling stream is crossed on a
small bridge and, 1.5km further
on, you again enter the National
Park and pass **La Puncha** on a U-
bend (🍴; see map page 89) — the
only picnic spot with a table. This
is also where you should park for
Walk 15.
Suddenly you are at **Madone de
Fenestre★** (39km ♦), a chapel
and the few houses of the French
Alpine Club. The magnificent
cirque shown on pages 8-9 rises
before you, dominated by snow-
capped **Mt Gélas**. In summer, the
chapel with its pretty frescoed
walls holds the 12th-century statue
of Notre-Dame-de-Fenestre, the
object of monthly pilgrimages; in
September she is returned to the
church at St-Martin (Walk 15
follows this pilgrims' route for
part of the way). Walk 14, steeped
in history, climbs from here to the
Italian border.

*Return to **St-Martin** (51km). Turn
left on the main D2565, pass the
plane-shaded parking area, round
the U-bend and now head south,
retracing day one of the tour.
Beyond **Roquebillière** bear left on
the D71 for BELVEDERE.*

Winding up into Belvédère, ignore
two small roads off to the right
just before the village. It's worth
turning left into **Belvédère** for the
view★ (66km *i* 📷) from the post
office: you look over the burgundy
stone village just below you and
down the terraced Vésubie Valley
east to the Turini Forest. There is
an excellent tourist office here,
with a small library.
From Belvédère continue north up
the **Vallon de la Gordolasque★**;
the road (now numbered D171) is
amply wide *at first*, but it will
narrow and become increasingly
difficult. From the outset, the
surprising absence of pines makes
this valley — our favourite — very
different from the Boréon and

*Consider spending at least half a day on the glorious pasturelands of the **Authion**, picnicking, sunbathing, and exploring the ruins. Even if you are not a military history buff, this incredibly beautiful green mountain (see also photograph page 84), riddled with old fortifications, will take your breath away.*

A natural fortress, because of its steep sides and strategic location on the border with Italy, the Authion has twice been the scene of bloody battles. Just after the birth of the French Republic, troops of the Austro-Sardinian coalition occupied the summit, and all Republican efforts to take it failed … until Napoleon took charge. Encircling the mountain with troops (30,000 men were involved in this conflict!), he cut off the enemy's supply lines — a successful strategy, which won the County of Nice for the Republicans. In World War II the Authion was the last place in France to be liberated, only two weeks before the end of the war, after heavy bombardment and a battle lasting three days.

Leaving the Col de Turini on the D68, after 3.5km you come to a monument to those killed in both battles. Bear right at the fork here and follow the one-way circuit, with magnificent views over the Bévéra Valley. There are information panels near the Cabanes Vieilles. When you reach a second monument, park and walk to the fort at the Pointe des Trois Communes, from where you will have a magnificent view over the deep Cairos Valley, towards the Mercantour and Italy. This fort saw the last battle of the Authion; it was taken, surprisingly, by five sailors. When you get back to the war memorial at the start of the circuit, continue back to the Col de Turini and then bear right on the D70 for La Bollène.

Fenestre. You climb in a bucolic setting past birch and chestnut trees, orchards, and walls built from the gorgeous local mauve-to-purple stone. Be prepared to stop for cows or sheep being led to pasture. Some 7km up from Belvédère, just after crossing a small bridge, look left to the lovely **Cascade du Ray** (☎). Another bridge is crossed about 1km further on; behind it there is a fine view ahead to steep snow-capped peaks, as the valley opens out. The hamlet of **St-Grat** (✕) greets you 2.5km further on, in the setting shown on page 92; its pretty modern chapel is on the left. As you continue below the Cime de la Valette on the left and the Cime du Diable on the right, the valley opens out into wrinkled grassy pastureland strewn with rocks, where the ribbon of river sparkles like tinsel. Just after passing a well-

concealed power station, the road ends at a parking area by the bridge shown on page 91 (**Pont du Countet**; 79km; 'Pont des Gravières' on Michelin map 115). Early in the morning, when the dew drops on the pastures shimmer like diamonds and you are likely to have the rushing stream all to yourself, this valley is an earthly paradise. Walk 16 begins just to the left of the bridge. Beyond the **Mont du Grand Capelet** rising due east lies the fascinating **Vallée des Merveilles**, where there are more than 30,000 rock engravings dating from the Bronze Age. The valley is an open-air museum, signposted with information panels by the National Park (see 'Note' in the right-hand column on page 91).

Leaving the bridge, return to the D2565 and bear right, back to **St-Martin-Vésubie** *(107km).*

Tour 3: UTELLE AND THE GORGES DU LOUP

St-Martin-Vésubie • Madone d'Utelle • Gorges de la Vésubie • Gorges du Loup • Gourdon • Thorenc

200km/124mi; about 7h driving; Michelin map 84 or 245, or larger-scale map 115

Walks en route: 17, 18

Roads are good, but narrow and winding. However, a 4.5km-long stretch to Madone d'Utelle is very precipitous and not recommended for nervous drivers or passengers. Avoid this road and the road in the Gorges du Loup on Sundays and holidays. Fill up with petrol before leaving St-Martin (the station is just north of the centre).

Picnic suggestions: *Don't* hope to picnic in the Gorges du Loup; there are very few lay-bys in the prettiest parts of the gorge, and it is always crowded. **Madone d'Utelle** stands on a high plateau with a panoramic view — perfect for picnicking, but note: the road to this chapel is *exceedingly narrow* for a short distance; there is little shade and, sometimes, in early autumn, this high ground is populated by more giant ants and crickets than a science fiction film. About halfway through the tour, on the D2 beyond **Coursegoules**, an oak-shaded stretch of road is extremely attractive, and there are grassy terraces to sit on. **Gourdon**, closer to the end of the tour, is the setting for Walk 17: follow it downhill for only five minutes, to a rocky ledge at the top of the trail just visible in the photograph on page 94. There are rocks to sit on, and some shade; the views are just astounding. The **Plateau de Calern** is crossed near the end of the tour; it's especially beautiful in spring when the wild flowers are in bloom, and you can park almost anywhere off the side of the wide road (D12). At the end of the tour, two fine choices along the D2: the old ruined village of **Gréolières** and the **Castellaras** (Walk 18), the panoramic viewpoint shown on page 95.

Leaving the pines and sparkling Alpine air of the Mercantour, we head south to the Grasse Pre-Alps, past terraced olive groves. From the *table d'orientation* above Utelle we enjoy one of the finest views in Alpes-Maritimes, before plunging into the Gorges du Loup.

Head south from **St-Martin-Vésubie** on the D2565.

You pass below the mellow spread of La Bollène. At **Lantosque** you cross the Vésubie, continuing on the D2565 (⌚🍴 on the left, just before a tunnel).

At **St-Jean-la-Rivière** (24km) turn right on the D32 for UTELLE.

The road climbs in hairpins past drystone walls terracing ancient olive groves. Just as you approach the old fortified village of **Utelle** (32.5km ♦🍴), there is a breath-taking view up the Vésubie Valley to the Mercantour, where the promontory village of La Bollène cuts into the valley like the prow of a ship. Park opposite the main gate, at the railed viewpoint, and walk into the village, to see St-Véran with its fine bell-tower and the charming White Penitents' Chapel.

Then continue uphill, after 1km going left at a fork for MADONE D'UTELLE.

After another 1.5km the road narrows to one threadbare lane. Park at the pilgrimage chapel of **Madone d'Utelle** (39.5km ♦). Legend has it that Iberian sailors, floundering in high seas off Nice, looked up to these heights and saw a light which guided them safely to shore. They founded the chapel in 850, but it was rebuilt in 1806. From here continue ahead to the domed *table d'orientation* ★ (☞), where a wonderful panorama unfolds — from the Alps via the Authion (just behind the chapel) down to Nice, off to Corsica, round to the Esterel and then north over the Grasse Pre-Alps.

Return to the main D2565 (56km) and turn right.

Continue along the steep-sided **Gorges de la Vésubie** ★, beside the bounding teal-blue river (various ☞; photograph page 17). Some 2km along, just beyond a tunnel, notice the exceedingly sheer walls on the far side of the gorge (the 'Saut des Français'): in 1793 guerillas from the County of Nice hurled Republican troops over these cliffs, just before Nice was reunited with France. Further on, where the Vésubie empties into the river **Var**, Bonson's church rises on the right, at the edge of a pyramidal hill.

*Go left for NICE on the N202, and cross the Vésubie on the **Pont Durandy**, with the wide pebbly Var on your right. Some 2.5km along, beyond **Plan-du-Var**, turn right for GILETTE on the D17, crossing the **Pont Charles-Albert**. At the T-junction, go left on the D2209 for CARROS.*

The road curls round to where the **Esteron River** also unburdens itself into the Var. At the confluence there is a superb view of the river basin, but nowhere to park. Just before crossing the Esteron, look up ahead to the perched village of **Gilette**. The pretty little lane climbs through pines and oaks. Soon you pass below the perched village of Le Broc and then go through a short tunnel below Carros.

Just past the tunnel, turn sharp right uphill on the D1 for CARROS

Madone d'Utelle

VILLAGE and LE BROC. At the next forks (in quick succession), go right, right again, then left.

These manoeuvres take you to the *table d'orientation* in old **Carros** ★ (81km ■☞), a gorgeous little village surrounding a 13/16th-century château and a windmill. From here there is a fine view ahead to Le Broc and towards the scattered perched villages on the east side of the Var. Below, the river fans out round little islets of white pebbles, all the way back to the broad basin where the Var and Esteron converge.

Leave Carros on the D1 for LE BROC.

There's a Mediterranean aroma to the air around here, where scented pines cohabit with aloes, and exotic flowers spill out over balconies and terraces. As soon as you enter **Le Broc**, bear left at a Y-fork for BOUYON (still the D1), leaving the 16th-century church spire off to the right. As you leave, pull up at a lay-by on the right just beyond the cypress-studded cemetery (☞): there are fine views over the Var and the **Chaîne de Férion** beyond it from this cliff-hanging perch. Some 2km from Le Broc, take in one final awesome view (☞) over the industrialised valley and up to Utelle, as well as perched villages left, right and centre.

23

Then the road goes through an oak wood and the views are lost until, 2km further on, Bouyon is seen across the valley. You cross the river Bouyon and go through the hamlet of **Les Moulins**. Entering **Bouyon** (93km), keep on the D1 for ROQUESTERON, ignoring the left turn up into the village, with its red-roofed church tower and wrought-iron bell-cage.

At a fork, keep straight ahead for BEZAUDUN on the D8, skirting the Bouyon on the left.

Beyond **Bézaudun-les-Alpes**, which rises off to the right, abandoned terraces flank the road. Ignore two roads up right into Coursegoules; keep to the D8 for GREOLIERES and VENCE, passing verdant rolling fields off to the left.

*After crossing a bridge over the river **Cagne**, turn right for GREO-LIERES, THORENC on the D2.*

Look left now for a fine view back to Coursegoules, where the 12th-century Romanesque church rises above grassy terraces. Shaded by oaks, this lovely grass-lined stretch of road is very pleasant for picnicking. Soon you look ahead to **St-Pons**, with the bald white summit of Cheiron behind it. The road passes below this hamlet.

At a junction with the D3 to Pont-du-Loup, go right, to keep on the D2 for GREOLIERES, THORENC. Then, just 1km further on, bear left on the D703 to CIPIERES.

The road descends in hairpins into the lovely **Loup Valley**, where verdant fields blanket the steep mountainsides.

At a fork after 2.5km, turn right and cross the river.

Now the walls of the gorge are glimpsed through graceful oaks on the left as you climb. The honeyed huddle of **Cipières** (121km), below a 13/18th-century castle, fans out nicely on the right. Just outside the village you pass the **St-Claude** chapel on the left; although badly restored and gaudily painted, it has a lovely wrought-iron gate. The dramatic road descends again, into a wide, open gorge of honey-coloured rock filled with trees. When the D3 comes in from behind and to the left, continue straight ahead for GOURDON. *Just under 2km along* pull over right at a lay-by on a hairpin bend: opposite you will find a very old signpost, 'Surplomb des Gorges du Loup'. Follow this short path to a railed balcony (📷), from where the view★ plunges over 350m/1150ft straight down into the Gorges du Loup.

Now go back the way you came for 2km and, at the junction, bear right with the D3 (GREOLIERES, BRAMAFAN).

You descend into the **Gorges du Loup★**.

Just before Bramafan bridge, turn sharp right, to skirt the river on a narrow two-lane road (D6).

Under 2km along pull up left to a terraced café, to see the **Saut du Loup★**, where the Cascade des Demoiselles foams into a huge

Cascade de Courmes, in the Gorges du Loup

pothole (nominal admission charge). From here the road goes through a tunnel, then descends through a bower of trees, where high orange-white cliffs tower overhead. You cross the **Pont de l'Abîme** in an invigorating setting, and then go through a second, tiny tunnel. The pretty **Cascade de Courmes★** (photograph opposite) is just at the exit, but you must park about 200m further on and walk back. Then the road runs through a longer tunnel, passing the odd lay-by, but the drama is behind you.

*At **Pont-du-Loup** turn right on the D2210 for LE BAR-SUR-LOUP and cross the river.*

Look right to see the pillars of the old bridge, destroyed in World War II. (*At this junction the D2210 heads east to Tourrettes and Vence, but these busy villages are best visited early in the day, direct from the coast.*) When you enter **Le Bar-sur-Loup★** (*i✝🅼🎦*) turn right to climb into the village. Park in front of the huge, squat 16th-century tower (tourist office). Visit the 15th-century Gothic church, with its beautifully-carved south door. At the left of the church is a magnificent viewpoint over the Loup Gorge.

*Continue south on the D2210 and, at **Châteauneuf-Pré-du-Lac**, go right on the D3 for GOURDON.*

Now the D3 affords splendid views (🎦) to the Loup Gorge, Le Bar and magnificently-sited **Gourdon★** (153km *i🅼*M; photograph page 94). Park below the village, where Walk 17 begins and ends.

From Gourdon head west on the D12.

The wide, little-used road climbs to a plateau, with fine views (🎦) back over Gourdon and down to the coast.

Ignore a narrow road off left to Les

Claps* but, at the **Col de l'Ecre**, turn sharp left.

After 3km the road makes a sharp left turn; you pass below an observatory and cross the **Plateau de Calern** on a wide grass-lined road, a delight of wild flowers in spring.

*Follow CAUSSOLS at the next fork and, beyond **Caussols**, bear right. When you meet the D5 go straight ahead for THORENC, GREOLIERES.*

From the **Col de la Sine** (🎦) there are spectacular views towards the bright-white **Montagne de l'Audibergue**.

*When you cross the **Pont-du-Loup**, ignore the road straight ahead for Andon. Turn right for THORENC, GREOLIERES, then fork right on the D79 to Gréolières.*

Skirting the Loup, this road takes you to the attractive village of **Gréolières**.

Outside Gréolières head back east on the D2 for THORENC.

Just above the village there is a splendid picnic spot, at the ruins of the original hamlet. This magnificent high-level road above the Loup Valley is a dramatic run through tunnels laced with viewpoints (🎦). Some 7km along you have the option of a 22km return detour to the summit of **Cheiron**. Note the D5 coming in from the left just past the Cheiron turn-off: 0.6km futher on, you could park on the left for Walk 18.

*Take the next right turn, the D502, into **Thorenc** (200km).*

---

*This is an even more attractive route across the plateau than the D12, but is *very narrow* (avoid on Sundays). You could follow it via **Les Claps** back to the D12. At the D12 turn right towards CAUSSOLS, but then fork left at the next junction (D112), to rejoin the tour on the D5 towards THORENC.

Tour 4: IN NAPOLEON'S FOOTSTEPS

**Thorenc • Mons • Fayence • Bargemon • Gorges de Pennafort •
Bagnols-en-Forêt • St-Cézaire-sur-Siagne • St-Vallier-de-Thiey •
Route Napoléon • Thorenc**

*203km/126mi; about 8-9h driving;
Michelin map 84 or 245, or larger-
scale map 114*
Walks en route: 18-22
*All the roads are good, but some are
narrow. On a short stretch of single
lane road between Callian and
St-Cézaire there are few passing
places. Fill up with petrol at Thorenc
or Fayence.*
Picnic suggestions: About halfway through the tour you come
upon a red-rock landscape remin-
iscent of the Esterel; it runs
between the **Pennafort** and
Blavet gorges. The best picnicking along this 17km-long stretch is
just after you cross the river
Endre, in a setting of parasol pines
or cork oaks. Just at the end of the
tour, the chapel of **Notre-Dame-
de-Gratemoine** on the Route
Napoléon is a superb setting for an
evening picnic (cover photograph).

While this circuit in the Grasse Pre-Alps takes in some
fine perched villages and pretty gorges, two landscapes
are likely to linger in your memory: the red-rock world
beyond Pennafort and your ascent of the magnificent Route
Napoléon below the white Malay, Lachens and Audibergue
mountains. Below the village of Séranon you come upon the
brave old chapel shown on the cover, standing in total isolation below the glowering heights of Bauroux. The austere
beauty of this setting, especially at sunset, is overwhelming.

From **Thorenc** *take the D2 east
towards GREOLIERES.*

The relay on the Col de Bleine is
seen up to the left, while ahead on
the right an old ruin rises on a
thimble of rock. Watch for a small
iron cross on the right 1.2km
along; 200m further on you could
park for Walk 18, to the ruined
Castellaras atop the rocky crag.

*Just 0.6km further on turn right on
the D5 for ANDON.*

At the **Col de Castellaras** (📷)
there is a fine view along the Loup
Valley and over to the snowy-
white Audibergue.

*Turn right on the D79 for ANDON
and SERANON. Beyond* **Andon**
continue towards CAILLE (still D79).

Ahead is an appealing, 'sugar loaf'

Mount Lachens from the N85 (Route Napoléon)

Mons (top) and Callian

mountain — the eastern flanks of the mighty **Bauroux**. When you are just below it, at a fork, keep straight ahead into **Caille**. Walk 22 drops down into Caille (literally) after storming the Bauroux summit, but Short walk suggestion 3 on page 101 is a delightful, easy ramble from Caille.

Keep following GRASSE, RN85 until you reach the N85 (20km). Turn left for GRASSE; then, 2.5km along (at the Col de Valferrière), go right on the D563 for MONS.

The limestone edge of the **Audibergue** rises on the left here, and you look ahead to the **Montagne de Malay**. Soon you enter **Var**, and a verdant basin opens up ahead below **Lachens**, the mountain shown opposite. Pines and oaks accompany your descent into the **Vallon du Fil** until, just before Mons, you enjoy a fine view across terraces to the Audibergue and down right to the village. Lovely grassy fields and plane trees welcome you into **Mons★** (35.5km *i✝🖾*). Park in the main square with its 18th-century fountain, tourist office and *table d'orientation*, from where there is a superb view down over the Siagnole Valley (Walk 19). The Audibergue rises to the left, and the vista sweeps round past the high-rise flats in Grasse to the Alps and — on clear days — across the Mediterranean to Corsica. Leave Mons the way you came in, passing to the left of the 15/17th-century church with its bell-cage.

Just as you are leaving, turn right (not signposted, but there is an old sign ahead on a wall, GROTTES DE ST-CEZAIRE).

Soon after this turn, pull up right opposite a chapel, from where there is a fine view back to Mons. You are now on the D56, a pretty little road zigzagging through holm oak, with views down to the Mediterranean.

After 4.5km keep right with the D56, where the D656 goes left to St-Cézaire.

Terraced hillsides splashed with fig trees and olives groves grace this single-lane road, as you head towards the Montagne de Malay. If you are planning to do Walk 19, park just before the bridge over the Siagnole (some 2km from the St-Cézaire turn-off). Otherwise continue over the bridge and, 0.5km further on, watch out on the left for a sign alerting you to the **Roche Taillée★** (*🏛*; photograph page 133). There is no parking here; you must pull up where you can and walk back.

At a fork, turn right on the D37 (signposted to the D563).

The road passes to the left of the **Château de Beauregard**.

On meeting the D563, turn left for FAYENCE.

As you approach the village, you are heading straight for the Esterel, and spikes of cypresses pierce the landscape. You pass to the right of the 18th-century classical church in the large village of **Fayence** (55.5km *i*). Follow TOUTES DIRECTIONS. As you curl downhill out of Fayence (*🥤*), there is a beautiful view to the right over fields.

Watch for your turn-off right (D19) to SEILLANS, 2km beyond Fayence; it's not obvious.

Beyond the Romanesque chapel of **Notre-Dame-de-l'Ormeau** you come into the pink- and honey-hued village of **Seillans** (*i*✚⛪), with an 11/15-century Romanesque church and a castle.

From Seillans take the D19 towards BARGEMON.

There are fine views over a series of green basins. Then a lovely forest of oak and sweet-scented pines takes you almost all the way to **Bargemon** (75km *i*✚⛪). This ancient village is a good place to shop, amidst the shady squares and bubbling fountains. Take time, too, to see the 12th-century fortified gates, 15/17th-century church, the ruined castle, and the 17th-century chapel of Notre-Dame-de-Montaigu with its Gothic spire.

From Bargemon follow CALLAS (D25).

There is a good view to the houses sheltering below the ruined castle on your approach to **Callas** (*i*⛪), from where you follow *LE MUY* (still the D25), skirting vineyards on the right and crossing the D562.

Just beyond a small lake and waterfall on the left, opposite a hotel, the red-rock **Gorges de Pennafort**★ rise on the left. The next 17km take you through some of the most beautiful landscapes in the region, with frequent lay-bys (🅿) and places to picnic. Although this area isn't mentioned in most tourist guides, wine-lovers flock to the various *domaines* en route (photograph below), to sample their Côtes de Provence.

At the D47, go left for BAGNOLS.

Beyond a forest of graceful umbrella pines, you cross the river **Endre** and come into a 'museum' of cork oaks, from where there are fabulous views down to the coast. The rosy brushstrokes culminate in a final flourish at the **Gorges du Blavet** (Walk 20), beneath stipples of purple-flowering heather and metallic-leaved holm oaks.

Soon Bagnols spreads out ahead on the right. The access road to Walk 20 turns off to the right at the **Chapelle Notre-Dame** (⛪), just before the wine cooperative.

At a junction, turn left for FAYENCE.

You climb through pretty plane-shaded **Bagnols-en-Forêt** (112km *i*) and leave it on the D4, with good views ahead to the mountains where the tour began — Malay, Lachens and Audibergue.

Ignore the D56 right to Callian; keep left for ST-PAUL-EN-FORET. In

Vineyard near the Gorges de Pennafort

St-Paul-en-Forêt, *keep right on the D4 for FAYENCE, GRASSE. After 5km turn right for GRASSE (D562).*

Soon there is a fine view ahead to the two square towers of Tourrettes, with Fayence to the left. The road skirts to the right of an aerodome.

Turn left on the D56 for CALLIAN.

Callian, crowned by its castle, now rises on a hill to the right, with Montauroux beyond it. Cypresses, olive groves and the salmon-coloured rooftops of scattered houses enhance the climb towards **Callian** (131km ✚🖶). You pass below the 15/17th-century château and to the right of the 17th-century church with glazed tiles on the tower.

Leave Callian on the D37 for MONS.

There is a lovely view of Callian down to the left.

Just over 0.5km along the D37 turn right on the D96 for ST-CEZAIRE.

Soon there is a fine view right towards St-Cézaire, as you start up the valley below the towering walls of the **Gorges de la Siagne★**, with the Audibergue ahead. Some 6.5km along you cross the Siagnole; ignore the D656 left to Mons here: keep ahead and cross the Siagne, at the same time entering **Alpes-Maritimes**. Now go down the other side of the gorge, at the base of the escarpment, on a good, two-lane road. Climb in zigzags through terraced olive groves into **St-Cézaire-sur-Siagne★** (144km *i*✚🖾), and follow CENTRE VILLE to park in this wonderful medieval perched village with a fine 13th-century cemetery chapel (Notre-Dame de Sardaigne, where Walk 21 begins). From the church you can follow a path to a *table d'orientation*. The famous **Grottes de St-Cézaire** are 4km northeast of the town, on the D613.

Leave St-Cézaire on the D5 for ST-VALLIER.

Again heading towards the Audibergue, you come into **St-Vallier-de-Thiey** (153km *i*✚🖶), a former Roman stronghold and a pleasant holiday resort. A 12th-century church is adjacent to the castle housing the town hall.

On meeting the N85 turn left for CASTELLANE.

This is the **Route Napoléon★**, climbed by the Emperor on his return from exile in Elba in March 1815, when he headed for Grenoble and an uncertain future. To avoid the main roads (guarded by troops loyal to the king), his small band used what was then a steep, muddy mule-trail. From the **Pas de la Faye★** (159.5km 🖾) there are superb views to the south, from La Napoule Bay to the Maures. Beyond **Escragnolles** the Audibergue peters out on the right, in a final curtain of cliffs. At the **Col de Valferrière** you pass the D563 to Mons, followed earlier. Drystone walls terrace the approach to **Séranon**, where you come upon the **Chapelle Notre-Dame-de-Gratemoine** (see cover). Short walk 22-2 can begin here, but the main walk begins in the village up to the right. Just 1km beyond the chapel, watch for Séranon's exquisite old post office, on the right (photograph page 1). Beyond here (🍴) the grandeur of the road ends in a jumble of touristic sites, shattering the illusion of marching with history. At **Le Logis-du-Pin** (186km) you cross the Artuby.

Turn right on the D2211 for ST-AUBAN; 2.5km along, take the D2 right for THORENC, GREOLIERES.

This *route touristique* skirts to the left of the clover-green **Lane Valley** (photograph page 102).

*After 13.5km turn left on the D502 to **Thorenc** (203km).*

Tour 5: LAC D'ALLOS

Thorenc • Castellane • St-André-les-Alpes • Colmars • Lac d'Allos • Colmars

123km/76mi; about 5h driving; Michelin map 81 or 245
Walks en route: 23; Walk 28 is nearby.
All the roads are good, but it's a slow pull up to the parking area for the Lac d'Allos (be sure you have enough petrol before starting on this road). Some passes may be closed between October and May.
Picnic suggestions: The **Lac de Castillon**, shown on page 113, is popular with picnickers, and there is ample parking by the dam or,

further on in the tour, at **St-André** (⋔). Beyond St-André, when you are skirting the Verdon, the ruined hamlet of **Font-Gaillarde** and the old bridge at **Pont de Villaron** (see opposite) are pleasant perches overlooking the river. But the best picnic spots on this tour are at the **Lac d'Allos** (photograph page 104) or the green slopes near the parking area, where the river Chadoulin weaves a meander through the meadows (photographs overleaf).

We edge one of the loveliest man-made lakes in the south of France, before following the Verdon upstream towards its source near the Col d'Allos. But the highlight of the tour is the magical setting of the Lac d'Allos — the largest natural lake in Europe above 2200m. Don't expect to see it from your car; it's a good half hour away. And while you're making the effort, *don't* just follow the crowds straight to the lake; do Short walk 23!

From Thorenc take the D2 west towards the N85.

The road skirts the Lane Valley on the left (photograph page 102). The 'sugar-loaf' mountain of Bauroux appears ahead (its summit, which towers above the Route Napoléon on Car tour 4, is the goal of Walk 22). Ignore the turning left to Caille; keep ahead past the hamlet of **Valderoure** and the pretty farm of **Malamaire** with its chapel.

Fork left on the D2211 for RN85.

After 2.5km you meet the Route Napoléon (N85; see Car tour 4) near the setting shown on page 26.

Turn right for CASTELLANE.

Just as you come into **Castellane** (34km; see notes on page 40), look out on the right for the beautiful 17th-century bridge over the **Verdon**. Then cross the new bridge and, if you are stopping,

take the second right turn after the bridge, to park in the Place Sauvaire.

From Castellane follow DIGNE and BARRAGE DE CASTILLON, to continue north on the N85.

The road climbs to the **Col de la Blache**.

At this pass go right on the D955.

Soon you begin to skirt the **Lac de Castillon★**, a gorgeous drive. Pull over at one of the large parking areas just before or after the 100m/330ft-high dam between this lake and the smaller, milky-green **Lac de Chaudanne** (☞ with information panels). At 42km you pass the C2 back right to Demandolx (Car tour 7 and Walk 28); keep ahead for ST-ANDRE, making for the salmon-coloured rooftops of St-Julien.

On meeting the N202, turn left.

You pass to the right of **St-Julien-du-Verdon**, a water-sports centre.

Ignore the road right to Angles; keep left, crossing the **Verdon** once more. Near the top of the lake, just as you enter **St-André-les-Alpes** (54km *i*), there is a large parking area (☎🏮) from where you can watch the paragliders based on the far side — below *robines* (clay slopes) running down the hillside in pleats. As well as being a world-famous mecca for paragliders, St-André is a fruit-growing area and a well-sited tourist centre.

Leave St-André on the D955 for COLMARS, COL D'ALLOS.

You soon cross the river **Issole**. This very pleasant road sees little traffic. As you approach **La Mure** the *robine*-etched valley of the Verdon is close by on the right. Beyond a stretch of woodland, about 10km from St-André, the valley opens out, with invigorating views of the rushing river and verdant fields running down off the mountains. With luck you'll spot the Train des Pignes (see page 130) along here, and give it chase!

After crossing the Verdon you are in the upper valley (various ☎), and green fields take you into **Thorame-Haute-Gare**. Some

2km further on, the impressive ruined hamlet of **Font-Gaillarde** on the left is a delightful picnic spot overlooking the river. Pass the Colonie de Vacances belonging to the city of Aix and, 2.5km further on, cross the Verdon yet again at **Pont de Villaron**. Just after crossing, look down right to a most beautiful setting — over the old bridge shown below. Should you wish to picnic here, pull over at the ruined building beside the road.

Having joined the D908, you enter a defile of honey-coloured cliffs and make straight for the snow-capped Alps (☎). After a straight stretch of tree-lined road, where false acacias and birches are prominent, you pass to the right of the pretty summer resort of **Beauvezer**.

Swiss-style chalets dot the landscape before **Colmars** (83km *i*✚🏛), which is approached along a lovely avenue of chestnuts. Notice the sundial on the Porte de France, at the southern entrance to this old fortified town. The parking area is further north on the main road; nearby are the tourist office and Fort de Savoie. The 16/17th-century Romanesque/Gothic church is near the gate with the

The old bridge over the Verdon at Pont de Villaron

Everyone rushes past the meandering Chadoulin stream (top) in their haste to get to the Lac d'Allos (shown on page 104), but it's a lovely place to linger. On the ascent to the lake, you look back across the Val d'Allos to the high mountains south of Gap (left). Short walk 23 diverts to a plateau below Mont Pélat (above), before reaching the Lac d'Allos.

sundial. As the road curves past the Fort de Savoie follow COL D'ALLOS.

False acacias line the road on the approach to **Allos** (91.5km). The heavily-restored 13th-century Romanesque chapel of **Notre-Dame-de-Valvert** is on your left as you enter (🕈).

Just 100m beyond the chapel, turn very sharp right on the D226 for LAC D'ALLOS.

Now you climb in hairpins past solitary farms, up the most westerly valley of the **Mercantour National Park**, towards the

32

pyramid of Mont Pélat. Rowans and graceful pines trace the Alpine landscape. The zigzags give fine views back over Allos, in a green basin backed by high mountains but, sadly, most of the old-style larch-shingle roofs have been replaced by corrugated iron. Beyond the **Ravin de Valplane** you enter the National Park, climbing beside the **Chadoulin** torrent. On reaching the parking area for the **Lac d'Allos★** (103km), turn to page 103.

*From Allos retrace your route back to **Colmars** (123km).*

Tour 6: GORGES DU CIANS

Colmars • Col des Champs • Beuil • Gorges du Cians • Puget-Théniers • Entrevaux • Annot • Thorenc

181km/112mi; about 5-6h driving; Michelin map 81 or 245; most of the tour is covered by larger-scale map 115.
Walks en route: 24-26; Walk 28 is on the alternative return route. *The tour follows many narrow winding roads; none is vertiginous, but you may have to back up a considerable distance if you meet oncoming cars. Some passes may be closed between October and May. Fill up with petrol before leaving Colmars.*
Picnic suggestions: You *could* picnic in the Cians Gorge, but only on one of the busy public walkways; this is disappointing, but there are other fantastic settings on this tour. Early on, the **Col des Champs** is a weird but incredibly beautiful setting of

robines (black clay slopes) covered with grass. There is no shade at the col but, beyond it, when you are below tree-line, you can picnic on grassy banks, under pines. At **Beuil** you could either follow Short walk 24 or picnic by the St-Ginié chapel, a short detour off the D28 (photograph page 106). Notre-Dame-de-Vers-la-Ville at **Annot** (Short walk 26) is a very pleasant setting with ample shade. As you approach Vergons, near the end of the tour, you will spot the apse of **Notre-Dame-de-Valvert**, a Romanesque chapel in a field on the right; it's a lovely setting, but there is no shade. If you take the alternative return route via the D102, consider an evening picnic at **Ville** (see Car tour 7 and Walk 28).

After an exhilarating run across high alpine pastures, we descend *the* most spectacular gorge in the south of France. Magical Entrevaux and three or four delightful walks lie en route.

Head north from Colmars on the main D908, then fork right on the D2 for COL DES CHAMPS.

The sign here, 'Interdit aux troupeaux', simply means that no livestock may be driven along the road; see *Transhumance,* page 133. This *very narrow* road climbs in hairpins; through the trees you can glimpse the upper Verdon Valley, pastureland and high mountains. Some 4km uphill you could park and walk to the **Panorama de la Collette** (30min return), a viewpoint over the Verdon and Lance valleys. Another 1.5km brings you to the **Site Nordique de Ratéry** (and a fine view left to Allos, then you continue through majestic pines. Before you've noticed it, the landscape changes totally, and you look left towards a 'bulldog's-face' of

furrowed slopes — grass-covered *robines* — weird, but incredibly beautiful pastureland (various). More charcoal-black clay slopes (see photograph on page 133) edge the road at the **Col des Champs★** (2087m/6850ft; 12.5km), from where there is a magnificent view to the encircling snow-capped peaks. Beyond the pass you leave Alpes de Haute-Provence for **Alpes-Maritimes**. The road (now two lanes wide and lined with gold grasses and mullein) descends below the needle-sharp **Aiguilles de Pelens** into the tree-line. Notice, 3km down from the pass, the sweet little chapel of **St-Jean** on the left, with its larch-shingle roof.

Just past the chapel, at a fork, go right on the D78 for LE MONNARD and ST-MARTIN.

33

This country lane threads its way past abandoned hamlets and neglected orchards. After 4.5km, where the D278 comes in from the left, there is a beautiful view of the upper Var Valley and the mountains behind it, as you approach St-Martin — seen down to the right through trees.

In the attractive resort of **St-Martin-d'Entraunes** *(28.5km) go right on the D2202 for VILLE-NEUVE, GUILLAUMES.*

The road, at first lined with fine-leaved poplars, crosses the river **Var**, then runs between orchards. Just past **Villeneuve-d'Entraunes** mountains and *robines* fall away to the left in tiers. Soon the Var is a mass of stones on your right, and you cross the river **Barlatte**. Beyond the hamlet of **La Ribière** lies the first of the tunnels (📷 at the exit) cut into the jagged mountain that dominates **Guillaumes** (40km *i☼*⌂), a very pleasant tourist centre with a ruined castle and Romanesque church.

*At Guillaumes go straight ahead on the D28 for ST-BRES, VALBERG.**

The good road traverses a chaos of rock, interspersed with pines and the occasional green field. Beyond the hamlet of **St-Brès**, at the **Col de Valberg** (📷) you look out left over the verdant basin of the **Alpreyt** stream and right over **Valberg** (53.5km *i*), a skiing resort best seen from a distance — or in the winter. Bear right in front of the church here for BEUIL, still on the D28. From **Les Launes** there is a good view right towards **Beuil** (☼🏠) — gateway to the Cians Gorge. There is a 15/17th-century church and Renaissance White Penitents' Chapel with a fine trompe-l'œil façade in the

village, where Walk 24 begins.

Leave Beuil on the D28 for GORGES DU CIANS.

Look back to Beuil's magnificent setting★ as you descend below tall flint-grey houses perched above Alpine pastures. Just over 1km along, a left turn leads to the St-Ginié chapel, where the photograph on page 106 was taken. Some 5km below Beuil you enter the red-rock landscape of the upper **Gorges du Cians★**. In its rushing descent of 22km from here to where it bounds into the Var, the Cians drops some 1600m/5250ft, leaving in its wake towering chasms. The most beautiful section of the gorge (and the longest) is the run between Beuil and Pra-d'Astier, where the river cuts through red schist. The contrast between the burgundy rock and the varying greens of the trees, ferns and moss is breathtaking. There is parking (📷) at all the tunnels; watch for signs alerting you to the **Grande Clue** and, not far beyond it, the **Petite Clue** — these are the most spectacular rifts. The red rock ends as abruptly as it began, just before the hamlet of **Pra-d'Astier**, from where you wind down below the steep cliffs of the Gorges Inférieures. Had you not seen the Upper Gorge, you would rate these honey-coloured chasms amongst the most impressive in the south of France.

At the N202 (82.5km), turn right for DIGNE, PUGET-THENIERS.

The road, lined with plane trees, follows the upper Var. On the approach to **Puget-Théniers** (*i☼*⌂), look up behind the castle ruins to the knife-edged **Castagnet Cliffs**; Alternative walk 25 tackles them in a surprisingly easy series of zigzags. Park in the small plane-shaded square on your right, near Maillol's famous statue, *L'Action Enchaînée*. Perhaps visit the old

*The Gorges du Daluis, south of Guillaumes, are definitely worth visiting when you have the time.

town and the 13/17th-century Romanesque church with its poignant calvary. Be sure to call at the excellent tourist office on the other side of the road, and the adjacent railway station, where you can collect timetables for the 'Train des Pignes' (see page 130) and the steam train. Walk 25 is a lovely circuit above Puget-Théniers. Plane trees on the right and a 5km-long tapestry of orchards on the left now take you to magical **Entrevaux★** (*i*✝▯), founded in the 11th century.

To appreciate the site (see overleaf), turn left opposite Vauban's gate, then go right on the D610 for PARKING PANORAMIQUE. Almost 2km up this road (where the C3 goes right to BAY), make a U-turn and drive back downhill. After 1km, at a bend, pull over to the right, by a stone bench (📷).

Back at the main road, park just opposite the gate (photograph page 131), go over the drawbridge, and explore the ancient village. Then continue west on the N202, skirting the Var. After crossing the **Pont de Gueydan** (where the Var has cut the Daluis Gorge on the right), keep left on the N202 for GRENOBLE, DIGNE, ANNOT. Now hemming the river **Coulomp**, you pass a viewpoint (📷) left over the old Roman **Pont de la Reine Jeanne**. A magnificent bluff rears up ahead on the right: Walk 26 would take you along its rim (see photograph page 110

At ***Les Scaffarels****, below the bluff, turn right on the D908 for ANNOT.*

The road follows the gentle green valley of the river **Vaïre**. On your right are gigantic boulders, the **Grès d'Annot★**; Walk 26 explores them; see photograph page 131. If you are doing that walk, turn right for GARE just before the centre. Otherwise continue to the main square in **Annot** (114.5km *i*) and park on the left to see the lovely old town.

Return from Annot to the N202 and turn right.

Under 2km along you edge the steep walls of the **Clue de Rouaine**. Beyond pretty **Rouaine**, the river **Iscle** flows below pleasantly-cultivated rolling hills, as you approach the **Col de Toutes Aures** (⛩) and the lovely Romanesque

Cians Gorge — the Grande Clue

chapel of **Notre-Dame-de-Valvert** (⛪). At **Vergons**, 2km further on, the **St-Ferréol** chapel perches atop a conical hill (notice its diagonal strata, so characteristic of this area). Beyond the defile of the **Clue de Vergons** you look ahead to the beautiful setting of St-Julien-du-Verdon on the **Lac de Castillon** (photograph page 113).

At the D955 turn hard left, retracing the outward route of Tour 5 back to **Thorenc** (181km). Or vary the return: 5km along the D955 fork left for DEMANDOLX (C2; the opposite direction to Tour 7; Walk 28 lies en route). Just before Demandolx, keep right on the sometimes narrow D102 above the Chaudanne Lake, rejoining the N85 east of Castellane.

Entrevaux was fortified in the late 17th century by Vauban, who linked the hilltop castle with the lower town, enclosing both in ramparts. You can climb to the ruined fortress for superb views over the village and the Var Valley.

Tour 7: RIFTS AND RIVER VALLEYS

Thorenc • Col de Bleine • Aiglun • Sigale • Clue de St-Auban • Lac de Castillon • Castellane • Comps-sur-Artuby • Tourtour • Aups

176km/109mi; about 7h driving;
Michelin maps 81 and 84 (or map
245), or larger-scale maps 114, 115
Walks en route: 27-30
Two stretches of road are precipitous
and not built up at the side: the 1km-
long climb to the viewpoint above the
Col de Bleine, and the D10 from Les
Sausses to Sigale. The D10 is only
recommended for very confident
drivers, as there are few passing
places. Avoid on weekends and in
July/August. Sound your horn, too, if
you feel uneasy: the locals do! Other-
wise, avoid this road altogether: when
you descend from the Col de Bleine,
turn left on the D5 for ST-AUBAN
rather than turning right for Le
Mas. The St-Auban clue is the most
impressive in any case, and you can
pick up the tour there (saving over
50km). No petrol between Thorenc
and Castellane (97km).
Picnic suggestions: There are
picnic places galore on this tour,
beginning with the **Col de Bleine**
(shade, rocks to sit on) at the start.
Our favourite setting in the *clues* is

below the **Pont du Riolan**, where
you'll see the 'Roman baths'
shown on page 38 — but you have
to be *very agile* to get down to the
river. Beyond Demandolx you can
follow Walk 28 for a short way to
Ville. Or picnic by the shores of
the **Lac de Castillon** itself
(photograph page 113), near
where you cross the dam (rocks to
sit on, shady trees 2km past the
dam). We inevitably make for the
settings shown on pages 6-7, 39
and 48, where it's easy to get
down to the **banks of the Verdon**
(just before the Clue de
Chasteuil). The chapels at **Comps**
(see pages 40-41) are an attractive
setting, but if you don't have time
to walk up to them, there is
another chapel just 1.8km south of
Comps on the east side of the
D955 (beyond a shrine). Near the
end of the tour, the 5km-long run
through the delightful mixed
woodland of the **Bois de Prannes**
is a good choice, especially if you
have a table and chairs.

This tour leaps from river to river, as we make our way
west to Aups. First we follow the Esteron and its surging
tributaries amongst the *clues*, the very deep and narrow rifts
they have sliced through the limestone. The kayakers are in
their element here, and you may have to compete with them
for parking space. We then move on to the Verdon and
perhaps picnic on its banks, watching more colourful kayaks
whizz by. But we don't venture into the Canyon (Tour 8)
today; instead we skirt its idyllic tributary, the Jabron. The
Artuby opens our route to the Nartuby and the pretty Gorges
de Châteaudouble. Late in the day there's one last chance for
a walk — from the delightful hill village of Tourtour.

Head north from **Thorenc**, to pick
up the D5 for COL DE BLEINE.

Look back now, down to Thorenc,
east to the ruins of the Castellaras,
and west to Bauroux.

Some 3.5km from Thorenc, at the
Col de Bleine (a popular hang-

gliding centre and very busy on
Sundays) turn right uphill on a
very narrow road; 1km further on,
go left (away from the relay).

The road ends at a superb view-
point★ (☎) south along the
Loup and Lane valleys (shown on

Be sure to pull up at the Pont du Riolan, a gorgeous picnic spot for those agile enough to get down to the river. Can you resist it? The white limestone basin with its sculpted strata and milky turquoise water brings to mind marble Roman baths. Kayakers are often seen here, where they meet up after navigating the Clue du Riolan.

page 102). In the northeast the relay at Madone d'Utelle stands out against the Alps of the Mercantour.

Descend from the viewpoint and continue over the pass, curling down to the Gironde Valley below the Montagne de Charamel.

At a junction turn right on the D10 for LE MAS, AIGLUN.* After 0.6km, at a Y-fork, bear right on the D110 for LES SAUSSES.

Round rock turrets rise on the left before you go through the attractive old hamlet of **Les Sausses**. Keep straight ahead on the D110 for LE MAS, AIGLUN.

When you meet the D10 again, turn right for AIGLUN.

The road narrows to a single lane. Now we begin our (sometimes hair-raising) circuit of the *clues*. As you approach the first of them, 3km along, there is a fine view to the right, over the village of Aiglun; beyond it, densely-wooded slopes rise on both sides of the **Esteron Valley**. Now you head in towards the rift, to a tight U-bend, where you cross the

*Or turn left on the D5, direct to the Clue de St-Auban, the easier route mentioned above.

38

Esteron. Although the road is *very* narrow here, if there is no traffic about, pull over. On your left is the blade's-width entrance to the **Clue d'Aiglun**★, an almost 2km-long gash running north between the Charamel and St-Martin mountains. Walk 27 begins at **Aiglun** (27.5km), the pretty eyrie shown on page 111 (top). It looks out across the valley to the Cascade de Végay and the Montagne du Cheiron.

Continuing east above the Esteron, you pass below Aiglun's cemetery, where the chapel of Notre-Dame rises on a promontory, surrounded by cypresses. The hamlet of Vascognes lies just below the road a little further on; Walk 27 goes through it. One can still cross the Esteron footbridge below Vascognes — in the invigorating setting shown on page 111 (bottom).

Now look ahead, to the perched village of Sigale, where the escarpment falls away in 'swirls' of strata down to the river. Some 5km from Aiglun, pull up just before or after crossing the **Pont du Riolan** (📷), to see the irresistible 'Roman baths' shown above. From here the road curves up to Sigale, cuddled into the ridge above the swirling rock. Its 19th-century clock tower, adorned with a bell-cage, stands out against the sky like a chess rook. Climbing through the olive-planted terraces shown on page 112, you join the D17 and go straight ahead for SIGALE on the good wide road that has come in from Roquesteron.

The Verdon at the Clue de Chasteuil (see also photographs pages 6-7, 48)

Come into **Sigale★** (37km 📷), a beige and pink sprawl of old houses shaded by planes. Two of the gates to this ancient fortified village are still intact, but what always catches the eye is the clock tower on its isolated rock plinth. You feel really high up here at Sigale, where the precipitous walls fall away to the confluence of the Esteron and Riolan.

From here a wider road takes you high above green fields to the entrance to the **Clue du Riolan★**, with a view left into this deep gouge across the mountains. Attractive pollarded acacias line the left-hand side of the road as you approach the **Pont des Miolans**.

After crossing the bridge, turn left on the D2211a for COLLONGUES, BRIANÇONNET.

Not far along, breaks in the dense foliage allow pleasant views to **Sallagriffon** up on the left. Behind it is the bulbous summit of Charamel. Soon **Collongues** reveals itself ahead, rising above verdant fields. As you enter, keep left for ST-AUBAN, GRASSE.

At the next junction, just over 1km further on, keep ahead on the D2211a for BRIANÇONNET, ST-AUBAN.

The old Roman village of **Briançonnet** (60km 📷) snuggles below a spit of rock with a ruined castle.

Keep ahead for ST AUBAN. Cross two bridges and, on coming to a Y-fork, go left on the D2221 for ST-AUBAN.

You continue in hairpins up to the **Clue de St-Auban★** (66km). Unlike the previous two *clues*, you don't just pass the entrance to this one — you drive *through* it for 1km (on a good, amply-wide road, with space to park and *savour* the drama). Park as soon as you go

through the first tunnel, to follow the railed walkway (📷) and look out at the massive vertical walls pitted with caves, and the boiling torrent below. (The photograph on page 132 was taken here, but there are other parking places *in* this clue and at the end of it, where there is also a café.)

Out of the clue fork right for ST-AUBAN; then ignore a road off right to the centre.

Still following the Esteron (D305), gentle tree-clad mountains rise on the left and a honey-hued rock edge on the right. On leaving Alpes-Maritimes for **Alpes de Haute-Provence**, the road becomes the D102, and rolling green fields suddenly appear on the left. Squeeze through the attractive pastel houses of old **Soleilhas** and keep straight ahead on the far side of the village for CASTELLANE. There is a gorgeous view back down to the Alpine setting of Soleilhas as you climb above it. On coming to the **Col de St-Barnabé**, go straight over for DEMANDOLX. This upland road, lined with gold grasses and wild roses, descends through *garrigues* towards the mountains behind St-André and Castellane.

39

Curlicued wrought-iron street lamps line the main road through **Demandolx** (83km ), from where there is a bird's-eye view★ down over the milky-green straits of the Lac de Chaudanne. (If you plan to do Walk 28, watch for the sign denoting the exit from Demandolx, and *take a km reading* there; you will want to park exactly 2km beyond the sign.) Not far below Demandolx, you join the C2 and keep straight ahead for CASTELLANE. About 0.5km after crossing an impressive road bridge, pull over to the left at the small iron **Croix de la Mission**. From this viewpoint★ () you overlook the breathtakingly-beautiful Lac de Castillon (photograph page 113), a turquoise mosaic of shadows and reflections. Beyond here, look straight ahead as you go into a deep U-bend: above rise the ruins of Ville, the setting for Walk 28 (park at the U-bend). Now the road curls down to the lake, coming to the D955 just above the red-roofed houses of **La Cité**.

Turn left on the D955 for CASTELLANE.

Under 1km along you come to the first of several parking areas ( and information panels) either side of the graceful dam between the **Lac de Castillon★** and the **Lac de Chaudanne★**. If you walk over the dam, you will appreciate its height (100m/330ft) — try not to think about the fact that it is only 26m/85ft wide at its base! Still skirting the lake, you pass some pleasant shady places to pull over for a picnic.

*When you meet the N85 (**Route Napoléon**; Car tour 4), turn left.*
In **Castellane** (97km *i*) the N85 heads towards the 14th-century Tour de l'Horloge with its lovely wrought-iron bell-cage and then turns right in front of it. Watch now, on the right, for house No 34, where Napoleon rested during his tiring slog up to Grenoble. Park in the central square just ahead (Place Sauvaire), if you plan to visit the town (one of the most popular touring and walking centres in Haute-Provence). It's a steep climb past the Stations of the Cross up to the early 18th-century pilgrimage chapel of Notre-Dame-du-Roc, but you will have a fantas-tic view over Castellane and the

Comps-sur-Artuby, with the St-Jean chapel (right) and the 13th-century Gothic church of St-André (left). Both are visited on Walk 29.

the road has been hewn out under cliffs and the river races by hard on the left. About 1km further on, you can park on either side of the road, and it's possible to get down to the river for a picnic in the gorgeous setting shown on pages 6-7, below the Cadières de Brandis. Beyond here the river curves to the south and soon the escarpment of Robion (photograph page 48) rises on the left. Then more cliffs arc over the road as you pass through another dramatic rift in the limestone, the **Clue de Chasteuil**.

*Bear left on the D955 for COMPS, crossing the Verdon on the **Pont de Soleils**.*

Soleils is a flower-bound hamlet in the shadow of Robion. Just past here, beautifully-pollarded chestnut trees appear on the right; they will accompany you all the way to Jabron. Soon **Trigance**, with its 16th-century château-hotel and church tower with glazed tiles, rises on the right (photograph page 45); keep ahead, soon following the green ribbon of the **Jabron Valley** on your right. On entering the mellow cluster of **Jabron** bear right for COMPS, still on the D955. You climb out of the valley, enjoying a wonderful view back over it 1km outside Jabron (📷). Then, 3km further on, there is another dramatic view — towards **Comps-sur-Artuby** (125km *i*), where the 13th-century Gothic church rises isolated on a hill, above more swathes of emerald cultivation. Walk 29 is a delightful short circuit from Comps.

Turn to map 84 now and, in Comps, continue ahead on the D955.

entrance to the Verdon Gorge. Don't miss the lovely 17th-century bridge over the Verdon (straight below Notre-Dame). Back near the clock tower you will find the tourist office and the 12th-century church of St-Victor. Castellane also marks the eastern end of the 'Route de la Lavande', which extends west to Sault (see *Western Provence*, Car tour 3).

From the Place Sauvaire turn right on the D952 for COMPS, MOUSTIERS.

As soon as you can, pull over to look back at Castellane's setting, for the fine view★ of the Virgin crowning Notre-Dame-du-Roc. (An *oppidum* once stood atop the rocky pinnacle, but the settlement spread down to the Verdon and was fortified in the 14th century; the clock tower is a remainder of those fortifications.) Now you skirt the glorious turquoise **Verdon River** on your left, past a string of camping and kayaking centres. Notice the 'crown' of dolomitic rock ahead on the right — the **Cadières de Brandis**. You pass the **Pont de Taloire**, a popular fishing spot, on the left, and then come to the **Porte de St-Jean**, a spectacular defile where

Just 1.8km south of Comps you pass a shrine and chapel on the left, with fine views left back to Comps and the valley of the Artuby (see photograph pages 40-41). Soon you enter a military zone dating from Julius Caesar's time on the **Plan de Canjuers**. Beyond the plateau the road winds downhill through pretty woodlands, where moss and ivy cling to the trees and stone walls. Ignore the road off left to the peach-coloured spread of **Montferrat**; keep right for DRAGUIGNAN on the D955.

Watch for the D54 left to Draguignan: ignore it but, just beyond it, fork right on the narrow D51 for CHATEAUDOUBLE.

This beautifully-wooded road threads below high cliffs on the north side of the river **Nartuby**, through the pretty **Gorges de Châteaudouble**. A short tunnel takes you into the old village of **Châteaudouble**. Beyond here you enter the **Bois des Prannes**, a beautiful 5km-long stretch of mixed woodland. Oaks predominate, but there are sprinklings of Mediterranean pines. In spring the road is aglow with wild flowers. Once out of the wood, verdant fields lead the eye to **Ampus** (155km). Squeeze through the

village, passing to the right of the well-restored Romanesque church with bell-cage.

In the village, bear slightly right for VERIGNON and, when you (quickly) meet a road crossing in front of you, keep right for TOUR-TOUR (D49). When the D49 goes right to the Gorges du Verdon, keep ahead for TOURTOUR (D51).

A pine wood takes you along to **St-Pierre-de-Tourtour**, a modern 'second-home' development. Holm oaks join the pines on the approach to the hill village of **Tourtour★** (163km *i🚻🏕️📷*), where the 11th-century church of St-Denis stands well off to the left (photograph page 116). Walk 30 begins here in the main square. The château now houses the *mairie;* the tourist office is nearby. After wandering the lanes to admire the beautifully-restored old houses, walk to the church, from where there is a brilliant view★ stretching from the Gulf of St-Raphaël in the east to Mont Ventoux in the northwest, by way of the Montagne Ste-Victoire and the Lubéron.

From Tourtour continue on the D51 for VILLECROZE.

The road runs through wide-open countryside with olive groves and farmsteads. Look up right to the square **Tour de Grimaldi** on a hill 2km outside Tourtour; it can be visited on Walk 30. Some 2km further on, you pass a path up left to a *table d'orientation.*

At a fork, keep straight ahead for AUPS on the D557; ignore the road left for Villecroze. At the next junction keep right for AUPS.

Life centres round the plane-shaded square in **Aups** (176km *i🚻🅿️M*), with its 15th-century Gothic church, cafés, tourist office and museum of modern art.

Clock-tower in Aups

Aups • Moustiers-Ste-Marie • Grand Canyon du Verdon • Aiguines • Aups

162km/100mi; about 7-8h driving; Michelin map 84 or 245, or larger-scale map 114

Walks en route: 31, 32

A very early start is recommended: although the tour is short, you won't average more than 15km/h in the canyon if you stop at most of the viewpoints. If you plan to walk in the canyon, you should ideally spend the night at La Palud or the inn at Point Sublime, breaking the tour into two days. (If you will spend only one day in this area, it might be best to avoid Moustiers; you will lose too much time in this crowded tourist centre.) Be sure to fill up with petrol before leaving Aups! All the roads are good, and none is vertiginous. From November to March, however, you might find the corniche roads closed because of rock falls or, more rarely, snow. This landscape is the most visited natural wonder between the southern Alps and the Pyrenees; try to see it outside high summer, and avoid weekends. Note: The banks of a river are defined with your back to the source; as the Verdon rises in the east, the rive droite (right bank) is to the north, and the rive gauche (left bank) to the south.

Picnic suggestions: The **Pont de Galetas** is our first, dramatic introduction to the Verdon at the mouth of the canyon. There is a large picnic site here (no tables), where you can rent a pedalo. A quieter place, where no one seems to stop, is the **Maison Cantonnière de St-Maurin** (one 🍽), on grassy slopes overlooking the river. Another gorgeous setting is the confluence of the Verdon and Jabron at the **Clue de Carejuan** (busy on weekends and in high season). By contrast, no one makes the effort to descend to the Roman **Pont du Tusset** (photograph page 121), so you would have this gorgeous setting all to yourself if you do Short walk 32.

The Grand Canyon du Verdon owes its name to the father of speleology, E-A Martel: 'We have here a real wonder, unique in Europe', he wrote; 'it is the most American of all the canyons in the Old World — and I've not changed my mind since seeing the Grand Canyon in Colorado'. It was Martel who first explored the depths of this 25km-long gorge, together with Isidore Blanc, a schoolteacher from Rougon. They set off on their three-day 'cruise' in August 1905 — in a rowing boat equipped with a wooden ladder and, it is said, dressed in overcoats and bowler hats (see also page 117). We urge you, too, to see the canyon from the river bed; its true grandeur can only be appreciated from the depths.

Leave Aups on the D957 north (LES SALLES, MOUSTIERS).

Just over 15km from Aups, pull over at the large parking area on the left (🕿) for a superb view★ to the **Lac de Ste-Croix** and Les Salles. In the morning the sun shines on the burnt sienna cliffs ahead — a perfect backdrop for the glimmering turquoise lake and red roofs of **Les Salles**. Skirting the lake on the D957 (🍽 at 21km, 23km), you pass the D19 off right; this is the main westerly access road to the south bank of the canyon (the 'Corniche Sublime'). Keep straight ahead for *MOUSTIERS.*

As you cross the Verdon on the **Pont de Galetas** (25km), look

43

Belvédère de l'Escalès (left) and the Tours des Trescaires (above). Notice how the different layers of sediment are clearly seen in these twin pillars — as opposed to the smooth compact limestone of the Escalès climbing wall on the left.

right for a fantastic view★ into the milky-green waters of the gorge. Just over the bridge, you are in **Alpes de Haute-Provence**; pull up in the large parking area (☎ with information panels; pedalo rentals), a perfect picnic setting beside the lake (but in summer and autumn beware: you may encounter a veritable cyclone of gnats and mosquitoes here). More good viewpoints are passed (☎) before you climb away from the lake along the valley of the river **Maïre**.
Ignore for the moment the D952 right to Castellane *(or turn right here, if you are not going into Moustiers)*; continue ahead to **Moustiers-Ste-Marie★** (32km *i♦M*). Overspilling with day-trippers, Moustiers is best seen very early or late in the day. Its magnificent setting cannot be appreciated from this approach; you must park outside the village and walk in. A chain with a gold
44

star is suspended between the cliffs dominating the village. High in a ravine, below the star, stands the 12/16th-century pilgrimage chapel of Notre-Dame-de-Beauvoir, from where there are fine views down over the rooftops of Moustiers and towards the Valensole Plateau. A wide walkway climbs to this chapel, past the 14 Stations of the Cross depicted in faïence. Moustiers grew rich on faïence during the 17th and 18th centuries and, while the industry declined in the 19th century, it has been revived today for the tourist trade. Unlike the tourist shops, the Musée de la Faïence contains only the finest examples of the art; it is next to the Romanesque church with its impressive four-storey bell-tower.

From Moustiers take the D952 towards CASTELLANE. Just 2km along, keep left on the D952, for LA PALUD, CASTELLANE.

The road climbs steadily towards the north (right) bank of the canyon, soon entering the **Forêt Domaniale du Montdenier**; here and there you can pull up for views back over the lake (☎). Watch out for the **Belvédère de**

Trigance, a good base for exploring the Verdon. If you visit in autumn, you may have the unforgettable experience of seeing a transhumance *(see page 133) in the village lanes.*

Galetas★ (📷), a large parking area on the right 8km up from Moustiers *(not signposted)*. This is your last chance to look back over the lake and down to where the jade-green flow of the Verdon escapes from the narrow straits. At this point you enter the **Grand Canyon du Verdon**★ and follow the right bank to the start of the canyon at the Clue de Carejuan. Throughout the tour the walls of the gorge will open and close like a bellows, in places narrowing down to only 200m/650ft across.
Just 1km beyond the Galetas viewpoint, you pass the old **Maison Cantonnière de St-Maurin** (🍴), a lovely picnic spot overlooking the river. The first abbey in Provence once stood on this site. Some 3.5km further on, beyond the Mayreste farm, a large parking area alerts you to the **Belvédère de Mayreste**. The viewpoint★ (📷) lies 300m/yds up from the road, to the right (watch your footing on the slippery path). From here you have a first good outlook upstream into the canyon. A seasonal café (☕), the Relais des Gorges, is passed on the right 2km further on. At the **Belvédère du Col d'Ayen** (2km beyond the café; *not* signposted) you have to walk

another 250m/yds to the viewpoint★ (📷), looking ahead to the deepest and narrowest part of the canyon, where the walls are under 10m/30ft apart at the base. The river is an incredible 535m/1750ft below you here.
Now the road turns away from the gorge, and you pass Les Chalanettes, a farm selling local produce — honey, goat cheese and the lavender which thrives on this chalky soil. Look ahead now to the beautiful spread of fields around La Palud and the still-distant pyramid of Robion, the mountain shown on page 48.
An 18th-century castle rises above **La Palud-sur-Verdon** (51.5km 🚶), an ideal base for walkers, where you will find guides, taxis, maps and provisions.

From La Palud continue east on the D952 towards Castellane, then turn right on the D23.

The road rises through fields of lavender and then a wood, to the edge of the canyon. You're now on the **Route des Crêtes**★ — a 22km-long one-way corniche road with no less than 16 superb viewpoints (📷); all have ample parking, but not all are signposted. Our favourites are highlighted below (see map pages 118-119).

45

The **Trescaïres** belvedere offers your first good view upstream towards the Samson Corridor and the inn at Point Sublime, with Rougon above it. Below you are the twin turrets shown on page 44, the 'Tours des Trescaïres'. From the **Belvédère de l'Escalès** the view plunges down over a magnificent climbing wall rising 500m/1650ft above the river. The **Dent d'Aire** (🍴) boasts the only 360° viewpoint on this road. At the **Tilleul** viewpoint, a dizzying 565m/1850ft above the river, you are just opposite the gash of the Artuby gorge and not far south of the Escalès climbing wall and the honey-coloured cliffs of the Dent d'Aire. You're unlikely to miss the **Gorge de Guègues** (photograph page 2), where goats loll about on the concrete 'casting couch'. These film extras will add scale to your photographs of the Plan de Canjuers in the southwest and Mt Robion in the east. From the **Belvédère des Glacières** there is a fine view to La Mescla (photograph below), where the Artuby flows into the Verdon, and the spine of rock enclosed in the meander of the Verdon.

The **Belvédère de Guègues**, on a tight hairpin bend, looks back to La Mescla and over right to a narrow corridor of rock called the 'Cavaliers'. Not much further along, you come to the **Chalet de la Maline**, from where Walk 31 descends to the Sentier Martel — the most popular footpath in the canyon. Just past the chalet, you catch the Verdon in one of its more tranquil moods, at the **Estellié Belvedere**. Finally, the belvederes of **L'Imbut** and **Maugué** offer exceptionally good plunging views into the gorge (now 'only' 300m/1000ft below you), but nothing is to be seen of the river itself — it's buried under a chaos of rock. Soon the road runs through a Swiss-Alpine landscape of rolling fields, and you come back to **La Palud** (76km).

Again head west on the D952 for CASTELLANE.

Away from the drama of the canyon, there is a fine view left into the **Baou Valley**, its emerald fields dotted with solitary farmsteads. Almost opposite the road up left to Rougon, pull over right at the **Point Sublime** (83km 🏔 ✕), *the three-star viewpoint on the north bank. After locking everything in the boot of your car,* follow signposting to the railed viewpoint★ (📷 15min return) above the confluence of the Baou and Verdon. Before you is the magnificent cleft of the Samson Corridor. Why not spend the night at the inn here, to enjoy this superb setting to the full? In the morning you can watch the mists rise over the canyon and then set out on Walk 31 or Walk 32. At the very least, *do* try to get down to the Pont du Tusset (Short walk 32; photograph page 121) or the Baume aux Pigeons (Short walk 31).

Continue ahead from the Point Sublime for 0.7km and then, just before a tunnel, turn very sharp right on the D236.

This road takes you down *into* the **Samson Corridor**★, where it ends at a large parking area — just where the river **Baou** flows into the Verdon. Walk 31 comes in here, after following the Sentier Martel from below the Chalet de la Maline, and Short walk 31 to the Baume aux Pigeons begins here. This is the easiest access to the gorge for walkers, which is why it is usually so *very* crowded (another good reason to spend the night at the inn and jump the queue!).

Return to the main road and turn right through the short tunnel.

Now the balcony road begins its descent towards the river. At the **Clue de Carejuan**, the entrance to the canyon, beautifully-coloured strata arc over the road, and the river surges by on the right. There is parking here on the right, for a picnic area across the **Pont de Carejuan**, a gorgeous setting at the confluence of the Verdon and **Jabron** rivers. You're heading straight towards the escarpment of **Robion**.

Turn sharp right on the D955 for COMPS.

You cross the Verdon on the **Pont de Soleils**. (Tour 7 explores the Verdon further east, between here and Castellane; Tour 5 follows it north towards its source above Allos.) Go through the delightful honey-coloured hamlet of **Soleils**, bright with seasonal blooms. Then round a bend to enjoy a first view★ of **Trigance**.

Take the next road right towards the village but, at the next fork (after 200m), keep left on the D90.

You pass to the left of Trigance (the photograph on page 45 was taken here).

From the Balcons de la Mescla, you look down on the confluence of the Verdon and Artuby 250m/800ft below.

At the D71 turn right.

At the **Col de St-Maimes** (☞), there is another fine view to Trigance, Robion and heights west of Castellane.

Here we begin our tour of the south bank (*rive gauche*), the **Corniche Sublime★** (not to be confused with the Point Sublime on the north bank). The twin **Balcons de la Mescla★** (109km ☞🅿) are two of the best lookout points in the canyon. From here the view plunges straight down 250m/800ft to the confluence of the Verdon and **Artuby** rivers, at a point where the Verdon describes a very tight meander around a knife-edge of rock (photograph pages 46-47). The Mescla ('mixture' in Provençal) is one of the most beautiful stages on the Sentier Martel, where the pebbly shores of the river are an ideal picnic spot. You can see the footpath on the north bank, running below the Route des Crêtes.

Pull away from the Verdon once again, this time above the sheer walls of the Artuby ravine, which is soon crossed on the **Pont de l'Artuby★**. This bridge is astoundingly beautiful for a modern (1947) concrete structure; it spans the river with a single arch. Pull up just before (☞) or after (☞🅿) crossing, to admire not only the

bridge, but the spectacular view into the very narrow Artuby gorge. As you enter the **Réserve Géologique de Haute-Provence**, the road skirts the edge of the canyon but, unfortunately, trees and a roadside barrier prevent stopping along this stretch. (For much of the way this corniche road does *not* hug the cliff-edge; you remain at some distance from the gorge and keep making forays to the viewpoints.)

The **Belvédère d'Avelan** (☞ via a path off left and then right, 400m in all) offers a good view of the Artuby and the juncture of the two canyons. When you approach the **Tunnels de Fayet** *be prepared to pull up* just beyond the first tunnel★ (☞)! This is one of the finest viewpoints on the tour, from where you can see the great cradle of the canyon, with the river flowing in from the northeast and downstream to the northwest. Beyond the second tunnel (entered immediately), the river widens out and the views are not as fine.

Then you head inland across moorland and gentle rolling hills, the most northly reach of the **Plan de Canjuers**. Park just before **Les Cavaliers★** (114km ⛰🍴☞): from the terrace of the restaurant the views take in the canyon upstream and down, but what

The Verdon near the Clue de Chasteuil, with Robion in the background

*Château and church at Aiguines.
There is a museum here devoted to the
old craft of wood turning, which once
gave employment to most of the
inhabitants. Box was used to make these
beautiful objects, because of its hard
wood, colour and delicate graining. In
the depths of the canyon, protected by
the cliffs, the shrub grew to perhaps
10m/30ft high, sometimes with trunks
up to 20cm/8in in diameter. Gathering
these prize specimens was dangerous
work. The box-cutters were veritable
goats, descending hair-raising paths
into the depths (or in some cases
abseiling down with ropes); they then
lived in caves by the river's edge for
months at a time. The cut trees were
floated down-river to where they were
taken by mule to Aiguines.*

most impresses are the 300m/
1000ft-high sheer cliffs below and
the proximity to the north bank
(legend had it that horsemen could
jump from one wall to the other in
a single leap, hence the name). Just
beyond here there is a similar outlook from the **Estellié** belvedere
(📷), from where you can see the
path descending from the Chalet
de la Maline to the Sentier Martel.
From here the road skirts the edge
of the canyon for some 3km —
one of the most impressive parts
of the tour, with fine views both
upstream and down, but with few
parking places. It's worth leaving
the car at one of the lay-bys and
walking along the road for a short
time. As you look upstream from
the **Falaise de Baucher**★ (📷), the
Verdon races through the
steep narrow defile, where it soon
disappears under boulders at a
rock chaos 400m/1300ft below
the **Pas de l'Imbut** (📷).
From the **Margés** viewpoint★
(📷) you look upstream to the tail
of the lake and the end of the
canyon, with the Valensole Plateau
rising in the west. Then the road
turns away from the gorge in a
wide arc, the **Cirque de Vaumale**.
At the **Source de Vaumale**★ (📷)
there are magnificent views to the
west — as far as the Lubéron and
Mont Ventoux — and north over
the viewpoints on the Route des
Crêtes. The Mayreste farm, where
the Verdon disgorges into the

lake, is seen below on the north
bank. The river is more than
700m/2300ft below you here.
This is the highest part of the
south bank road and, at 1200m/
4000ft, it's almost like flying over
the spectacle in a helicopter.
The helicopter landing pad at the
Col d'Illoire (📷) brings you
back down to earth: here you
finally leave the canyon. Enjoy a
last look at the rock walls, but you
will not see the river again. See if
you can spot the Montagne
Ste-Victoire in the west from here.
As you descend towards Aiguines
there is an excellent long view
(📷) towards the **Valensole
Plateau** across the lake; in autumn
its fields are a wash of russets and
golds. Soon the multi-coloured
glazed tiles decorating the four
towers of the 17th-century château
at **Aiguines** (134km ◼M⛽)
glisten in the sun, immediately
drawing your attention to its
proud setting above the lake, with
the church beside it on the left (📷
with *table d'orientation*).

*Leave Aiguines on the D71 for
MOUSTIERS. When you come to the
D957 turn left for LES SALLES, DRA-
GUIGNAN. Then follow this road all
the way back to* **Aups** *(162km).*

You pass an attractive war
memorial in the form of a broken
Greek column. On the left the
white strata of the Plain de Canjuers glisten in the low sun.

Tour 9: THE MAURES

Aups • Lorgues • Vidauban • La Garde-Freinet • La Croix-Valmer • Chartreuse de la Verne • Notre-Dame-des-Anges • Collobrières • Besse-sur-Issole • Carcès • Aups

243km/151mi; about 7-8h driving; Michelin map 84 or 245, or larger-scale map 114

Walks en route: 33, (34)

Because of the danger of forest fires, many of the roads in the Maures are closed to the public. This tour uses the only east/west road open to motor vehicles — the D14 on the middle ridge. Be prepared for very slow motoring in the Maures and on the St-Tropez Peninsula; roads are narrow and winding. The tour does not take in the famed Corniche des Maures (D559) because for much of the year it is a misery of traffic. If you come outside high season and can spend an extra day, do consider

driving the stretch from La Croix-Valmer to Bormes/Le Lavandou.

Picnic suggestions: The **D48** and **D558** at the start of the Maures circuit offer lovely picnicking under cork oaks or umbrella pines; one of the most picturesque settings is a bridge crossed at the junction of these two roads. There are also pleasant places to pull over on the **D14**, with views over the Périer Valley. If you were to detour to **Gigaro** (just before La Croix-Valmer), you could follow Short walk 34 and picnic under shady umbrella pines after about 15 minutes' walking (photograph page 124).

A part from the great beauty of its forests of oak, pine and chestnut, the Maures massif is fascinating for reasons both geological and historical. These are among the oldest mountains in France, part of a great continent existing during the Primary Era, some 500 million years ago. Today that continent lies below the Mediterranean, and all that remains of this crystalline land mass are the Maures and Esterel, and the islands of Corsica, Sardinia and the Balearics (as well as the Lérins, just off the coast). More recent history saw the massif as the first staging post in the invasion of southern France on 15 August 1944, when Allied forces landed between Hyères and St-Raphaël (see Walk 7). The French pushed west to Marseille and the Americans north to Grenoble and east to Nice; Provence was liberated in 15 days. For two massifs rising almost side by side, the Maures and Esterel could not be more different: where the Esterel is a jagged upthrust of red, the Maures present a more comfortable landscape of rolling fir-green ridges.

From Aups follow DRAGUIGNAN, heading south past the petrol station. After 0.5km fork left for VILLECROZE (D557).

Watch for the sign denoting the entrance to **Villecroze** and, 0.3km beyond it, pull over left into the municipal park, where a sign-posted path leads past a lovely high waterfall to some intriguing

16th-century cave dwellings (small charge for a guided tour). Continue beside the ivy-creepered walls of Villecroze and keep ahead for FLAYOSC, DRAGUIGNAN on the D557. Crossing a river, you pass two extensive *domaines*.

Where the D560 comes in on the right from Salernes, keep to the D557; then, 1.5km further on, go

right on the D10 for LORGUES.

It's worth stopping for a while at **Lorgues★** (22km *i♣*), to stroll along the plane-shaded square (one of the finest in the south of France) and into the pedestrian precinct; be sure to see the 18th-century church of St-Martin and the 14th-century walls.

The most straightforward way to leave Lorgues is to take the D10 south. But for a better view, leave by heading west on the D562 towards BRIGNOLES. Then, at a roundabout, take the third exit (LE MUY, LES ARCS, DRAGUIGNAN).

Now you have a lovely view left back to Lorgues, focussing on the church with its square bell tower and impressive buttresses.

At the next roundabout take the first exit, the D10 for VIDAUBAN.

The road heads towards the sweet little chapel of **Ste-Anne**.

After 3.5km bear right on the D48 for VIDAUBAN.

You descend through the oaks of the **Bois d'Astros** and pass the magnificent **Château d'Astros** on the right, surrounded by its vineyards and orchards; it once belonged to the Knights of Malta. After crossing the river **Argens**, you come into **Vidauban** (34km *i*), an ancient town which once traded in silkworm moths' eggs.

Leave Vidauban on the D48 for LA GARDE-FREINET.

The road passes under the railway and then the motorway. The landscape alternates between chartreuse-green vineyards and lovely stands of umbrella pines, with fine places to stop. The snakeskin-like trunks of these trees are fascinating, with their black and white diamond patterning. Note, but ignore, the D74 left to Plan-de-la-Tour: 2.5km further on you cross a bridge. This is one of the prettiest picnic settings, with a choice of umbrella pines or the river's edge.

The mairie at Lorgues — just one of the beautiful façades flanking the plane-shaded square

Just over the bridge turn left for LA GARDE-FREINET on the D558.

This lovely road through cork oaks, umbrella pines, and vineyards is usually *very* busy. We like to drive it on Sundays at lunch time, when it's virtually empty! Now the most northerly and highest range in the Maures rears up ahead. When the younger 'upstarts', the Pyrenees and the Alps, emerged in the Tertiary Period a mere 50 million years ago, their upheavals reshaped the existing land mass, creating the three parallel east/west ridges that today make up the massif. Unfortunately, today only the middle ridge is open to traffic, due to the danger of forest fires.

The red-tiled roofs of **La Garde-Freinet** (53km *i*⬚) are dominated by a ruined Saracen fort.

Leave La Garde-Freinet by keeping on the D558 south for GRIMAUD.

The road passes to the right of beautifully-kept **Grimaud** (64km *i♣*⬚), with its impressive ruined castle (you will have a lovely view of the setting later in the tour).

51

Leave Grimaud on the D14 for ST-TROPEZ but, 1.3km past the wine cooperative, turn right on the D61 (also signposted to ST-TROPEZ). Keep on this road when it curves to the right (where Port Grimaud is signposted straight ahead).

The road runs through vineyards edged by golden grasses and you cross the river **Giscle**.

At the N98, take the ST-TROPEZ exit from the roundabout (and note the km reading here; you must turn right 2.5km further on, at an easily-missed junction). Now keep following ST-TROPEZ, CENTRE COMMERCIAL.*

You pass the Centre Commercial on your left (*i*) and continue straight ahead past Luna Park on your right.

Now follow ST-TROPEZ and RAMA-TUELLE, but watch carefully for your turn-off right to GASSIN (D61;

---

*Or, to shorten the tour and avoid getting stuck in a traffic jam on the St-Tropez Peninsula, follow La Croix-Valmer here, and pick up the tour at the 96km-point.

2.5km from the roundabout with the N98).

As soon as you turn off, the village of Gassin rises straight ahead. Like La Garde-Freinet and Grimaud, Gassin was perched high enough to spot a sea-borne invader and far enough inland from the coast to enable the inhabitants to take defensive action.

Just over 1km along turn right for GASSIN on the C1.

The road climbs from flat vineyards into trees and past the substantial vineyards of Château Minuty on the left. You also by-pass the centre of **Gassin**, forking left outside the village and leaving it off to your right, above grassy terraces.

At a fork just outside Gassin, go straight over on the C2 for RAMA-TUELLE. At another fork almost immediately, go left, again following RAMATUELLE. At the next fork go straight on for RAMATUELLE (where a right is signposted to La Croix-Valmer).

After rising over the **Col de Paillas**, turn up left to park at the ruined **Moulins de Paillas**. From here there is a good view (🖼) over the vineyards of the peninsula and out to the azure sea. (The road continues for 1km to an old viewpoint shown on the Michelin maps; it was obscured by trees the last time we were there.)

From the windmills continue towards Ramatuelle.

Ramatuelle (82km 🍴) is a pink and honey-coloured village set above vineyards, with a 17th-century Romanesque church. The road passes to the left of the centre.

Follow TOUTES DIRECTIONS and then carefully follow LA CROIX-VALMER, turning right just beyond

Notre-Dame-des-Anges, dwarfed by the adjacent relay tower

the cemetery and then right again 2km further on (D93).

Climbing through umbrella pines, you enjoy a lovely view westwards as you crest the **Col de Collebasse**. Some 2km further on, from the **Hauts de Gigaro**, you look down left over the setting for Walk 34 — the beautiful stretch of coast shown on page 124.* The road continues to **La Croix-Valmer** (96km *i*).

From La Croix-Valmer go north on the D559 and, back at the junction by the Centre Commercial, turn left on the N98 for HYERES. Then take the D558 into COGOLIN CENTRE.

Busy **Cogolin** (107km *i*) is a nightmare to get through; *at first carefully* follow GRIMAUD at all forks, and note that Grimaud is usually signposted near *the bottom* of a mass other names.

Then watch carefully for your turn-off left for ST-MAUR and COLLO-BRIERES (D48).

Just past the *domaine* of St-Maur, with its tiny bell-cage, pull over right for a superb view across vineyards towards the twin towers of the ruined castle at Grimaud.

Turn left on the D14 for COLLO-BRIERES.

As you head up the middle ridge of the massif (the only ridge now open to motor traffic), the grass- and heather-lined road is beautiful from the outset, framed by cork oaks and rolling vineyards dotted with farms (📷). Soon the deep Périer Valley opens up on the left, cloaked in a thick mantle of almost-black trees. ('Maures' is derived from the Provençal *mauro*, a word applied to dark wood-

Cork oaks near La Garde-Freinet. Cork oaks flourish on the silica-rich soils of the Maures and Esterel, and they are assiduously cultivated for industrial use; most of the bark stripped from these trees will make bottle-corks.

lands.) You pass above the hamlet of **Capelude** (not on Michelin map 84), where the vines are espaliered. Then notice the reservoir below you (Barrage de la Verne), and the buildings on the far side of the valley — the Chartreuse de la Verne (📷), setting for Walk 33. Beyond the **Col de Taillude**, where you feel really deep in these velvety, oak-clad mountains, turn off left on a very narrow road (adequate passing places) to the **Chartreuse de la Verne** (132km ♦), a Carthusian monastery dating from the 12th century (open 11.00-18.00 in summer, 10.00-17.00 in winter; closed Tuesdays, November, Easter and Christmas Day). After your visit *do* follow Walk 33 for 10 minutes or so, to enjoy some superb views.

Return to the D14 and turn left.

Soon the typically-complex relay station atop Notre-Dame-des-Anges looms over the landscape like a hovering spacecraft.

If you are going to Walk 34, watch carefully for a left turn to GIGARO — the VC154, some 2.5km further on, and from there keep following GIGARO down to the coast. Park along the esplanade, just before the road turns inland.

Some 3km short of Collobrières, turn right on the D39.

The heavily-wooded road winds uphill towards the Col des Fourches, with brief glimpses towards La Sauvette on the right — the highest peak in the massif (and Var), at 779m/2555ft.

Just before the pass, turn left for NOTRE-DAME-DES-ANGES.

The old priory of **Notre-Dame-des-Anges**, remodelled in the 19th century, is rather dwarfed by the huge relay nearby. Through breaks in the trees, there are some fine views north towards the Alps and south over the Maures to the sea.

*Leave Notre-Dame the way you came but, instead of returning to the D39, head south on the forestry road (RFC1) down the **Vallon des Vaudrèches**. Back at the D14, turn right.*

Sweet chestnut trees surround **Collobrières** (168km), a market town specialising in chestnut delicacies, especially *marrons glacés*. The shaded square is one of our favourites in the south of France and an enchanting place to stop for a break; one of the cafés on the north side of the square has a terrace overlooking the fast-flowing river behind the houses.

Leave Collobrières on the D14 for PIERREFEU.

This road runs through the wide **Réal Collobrier Valley**, with far-reaching vistas of gently-rolling vineyards against a backdrop of dark green trees.

About 10km from Collobrières, watch for a sign on your right: PIERREFEU 2km. Just beyond it, turn right on the DFC1 (ROUTE DU VALLON DE MARAVAL).

You pass through vineyards and orchards, cross the Réal Collobrier and then go through the hamlet of **La Tuilière**.

Just outside La Tuilière, fork left (not signposted, but don't go straight ahead for Les Davids). At a

T-junction, turn left (where La Portanière is signposted to the right). After crossing the Réal Martin, turn right on the D13 for CARNOULES and PIGNANS.

Now the oak-clad lower slopes of the Maures give way to the vineyards of the **Réal Martin Valley** down on your right, protected by cane windbreaks and dotted with fruit trees.

Some 3.5km along, at a Y-fork, go left on the D13 for CARNOULES. Drive under the motorway, then keep right for CARNOULES. At **Carnoules** (191km) go under the railway and turn right on the N97, then turn left for CENTRE VILLE. In the exceedingly narrow streets of the village centre, follow BESSE-SUR-ISSOLE, to leave on the D13.

Beyond a beautiful *domaine* on the right, the flat stretch of road is punctuated by cypress spires and wind-bent planes. Keep heading north on the D13 from **Besse-sur-Issole**.

Cross the N7, following ABBAYE DU THORONET.

The N7 was the old Via Aurelia linking Italy with Arles. The D13 runs under the motorway and straight through **Cabasse**.

Beyond Cabasse, fork left for CARCES, still on the D13. (A right would take you to the Abbaye du Thoronet, a detour of 8km return.)

(The 12th-century Abbaye du Thoronet is 'sister' to the Cistercian abbeys of Sénanque and Silvacane visited in *Landscapes of western Provence* during Car tour 2.)

Soon the **Lac de Carcès**, beloved of fishermen and boating enthusiasts, sparkles on the left, and you skirt its banks for 4km to **Carcès**, where the **Gros Bessillon** rises in the northwest.

Follow COTIGNAC from Carcès, to keep on the D13.

The road crosses the **Argens River**, then the river **Cassolle**.

Entering **Cotignac** (☐), keep right (TOUTES DIRECTIONS). The D13 circles to the right of the centre. Climbing above Cotignac you pass to the right of the two ruined towers of the Château de Castellane.

Turn right on the D22 for AUPS. After 5km turn right for AUPS on the D560.

Sillans-la-Cascade is a lovely small touristic village.

At Sillans fork left for AUPS on the D22.

Soon a straight stretch of road affords brilliant views ahead, to the golden walls of the Grand Canyon du Verdon.

Turn left on the D31, back to **Aups** (243km).

Restful pastel façades and shady plane trees characterise the beautiful main square at Collobrières

Tour 10: LA MONTAGNE STE-VICTOIRE

**Aups • Lac de Ste-Croix • Tavernes • Rians • Barrage de Bimont •
Pourrières • Le Tholonet • Aix-en-Provence**

*164km/102mi; about 5h driving;
Michelin map 84 or 245, or larger-
scale map 114*
Walks en route: 35, 36
*The tour follows good, if sometimes
winding, roads. The road over the
Montagne des Ubacs is very narrow,
but not vertiginous. Fill up with
petrol at Aups or Tavernes.*
Picnic suggestions: Beyond
Jouques the gorgeous honey-
coloured farm of **Gerle** is passed
on the left. Just past it there is
parking space, where you can sit
on rocks, in the shade of pines.
Unfortunately, there is no parking
just a little further on where, in
spring, the most fantastic poppy
fields you are ever likely to see will
be in bloom. The **Barrage de
Bimont**, a huge man-made lake, is
ideal for picnicking (but can be
very busy on weekends and in high
season). The **Col des Portes** (⊼)
on the north side of the Montagne
Ste-Victoire is an impressive
setting, full of wild flowers. On
the south side of the mountain,
there are parking places under
pines all the way along the **Route
Cézanne** (photographs pages 4-5,
59 and 126-127). For something
intriguingly different, a really
shady grotto for a hot day, park at
Le Tholonet and follow Walk 36
for 25 minutes, to the ford by the
watercourse, where you can perch
atop the stumpy concrete pillars.

O f all the painters and subjects associated with the south
of France, Paul Cézanne's daunting struggle to capture
the essence of the Montagne Ste-Victoire comes first to mind.
Cézanne was born in Aix-en-Provence and, although his
father wanted him to study law, he was drawn to the arts. He
interrupted his studies to join Emile Zola, an old friend from
school days, in Paris. There Zola introduced him to some of
the leading Impressionists, who inspired his early work. But
he never felt 'at home' in Paris, nor with the Impressionist
School. He returned to Aix and developed his own style,
crafting luminous geometric planes to express form — a
precursor of Cubism. The Montagne Ste-Victoire became an
obsessive subject, and he painted it more than 50 times. You
can visit Cézanne's *atelier* in Aix (Avenue Paul Cézanne), and
the Musée Granet, which has a gallery devoted to his pictures.

Leave Aups by heading north on the D957 (LES SALLES, MOUSTIERS). Some 7.5km from Aups, take the D49 left for BAUDUEN.

The road runs between sweeping green fields. All at once you come upon the magnificent view★ shown opposite (☎), over the turquoise-green Lac de Ste-Croix. Bauduen is seen ahead on the lake, an attractive cluster of red roof-tiles; behind it is Les Salles and to the west the perched village of Ste-Croix.

Don't continue to Bauduen; turn left on the D71 for RIEZ.

Now skirting the **Lac de Ste-Croix★** (☎), you'll spot the little *belvédère* atop Notre-Dame-de-Baudinard on the hill to the left, by a farmhouse. In spring mauve-flowering valerian lines the road on the right, a fine contrast with the turquoise lake and its red-soil basin.

When the road forks, don't cross the dam to round the lake; keep left on the D71. (Or, if you don't plan to do any walking today, you could cross the dam here and take the 'Circuit touristique du lac', going via Moustiers-Ste-Marie and the D957, rejoining the tour at this point; add 58km.)

After 2km your road joins the D9: continue ahead, ignoring the road off right to Riez. As you climb (☎☂) away from the lake, swathes of lavender fields run off the road; you're at the heart of the 'Route de la Lavande', which extends west to Sault (see *Landscapes of western Provence*, Car tour 3). The road squeezes through the narrow lanes of **Baudinard-sur-Verdon**, a pretty village.

At the fork outside Baudinard keep right (again on the D71).

You may be surprised to pass a

Left: the Lac de Ste-Croix and Bauduen, from the D49

large breeding stable for horses, which would not have been out of place in the TV 'soap' *Dallas;* we call it Southfork. Attractively-cultivated fields take you to a junction 3km beyond the ranch: keep left here for MONTMEYAN. Now the road is straight for about 7km, and there may be military vehicles about; like the Plan de Canjuers, this area is used for army manoeuvres. After you cross the D271, golden cereal crops embroidered with wild flowers edge both sides of the road, a pleasant change from a surfeit of vineyards or lavender.

When you come to a junction with the D30, turn right for MONT-MEYAN. Just outside **Montmeyan** *you join the D13: keep left for LA VERDIERE, RIANS but, only 400m further on, go left for LE LOGIS, TAVERNES.*

You pass the turreted château of **L'Eouvière** with glazed roof-tiles.

When the D13 goes left to Draguig-nan, keep right on the D71 for TAVERNES.

On the left the **Château de la Curnière** stands amidst vineyards. Head straight through **Tavernes** (45.5km ☂☎), where an exquisite bell-cage rises atop the church tower (photograph page 10).

At the roundabout in front of the petrol station (your last chance for petrol for over 100km) go right on the D554 for VARAGES.

Leaving Tavernes you cross a flat agricultural plain, with good views to the twin Bessillon peaks in the southeast. At **Varages** (53km ☂) the Romanesque church has a multi-coloured glazed tile roof.

Keep following RIANS, to leave Varages on the D561 west.

Approaching **St-Martin**, its château rises on a wooded hill on the left. In **Esparron** keep straight on for RIANS, passing the faded-rose façade of the old wine co-operative — a lovely focal point for a photograph. Just outside Esparron, stop at the cemetery chapel of **Notre-Dame** on the left, covered with ivy and flanked by cypresses. Straight ahead is the **Montagne d'Artigues**, a conical hill. Mixed cultivation backed by gentle hills takes you to **Rians** (*i*).

Leave Rians on the D561 west for JOUQUES.

The Canal de Provence is now on your right. After crossing the canal you pass a gorgeous rose-tinted farm on the right, the **Mas St-Maurin**, fronted by a double avenue of planes and backed by the Montagne de Vautubière. Rounding a bend, you will be taken completely by surprise to find yourself in a tiny gorge, where you drive under a suspension bridge carrying the massive pipe of the Canal de Provence across the valley into **Bouches-du-Rhône**.

Just as you approach **Jouques***, go left on the D11 for VAUVENARGUES, SAMBUC. At a Y-fork, keep left on the D11.*

The road passes the cypress-studded chapel of **St-Antonin** on the right and a canal control centre. Now you see another gorgeous farm — **Gerle**, a cluster of honeyed stone on the left. Beyond it there is a pleasant pine-shaded picnic area with rocks to sit on. Another bend, and another surprise: you look down left over fields of poppies★ as far as the eye can see, a scarlet sea in spring. From here the narrow wooded road climbs the **Montagne des Ubacs**.

On cresting a rise, the northern flanks of the **Montagne Ste-Victoire**★ spread out in front of you — a brilliant sight. A shallow gorge takes you down through *garrigues;* while the river, on your left, is bone-dry, in spring this is a

delightful run, when the pale new shoots on the holm oaks glitter like olive leaves against the older, dark green foliage.

On meeting the D10 (96km), turn right.

You pass above **Vauvenargues** (■). There is ample parking on this main road (☎), from where you can photograph the 14/17th-century château below in the village, where Picasso lived from 1958 until his death — and where he is buried. It rises above a small chapel, in a setting of exceptionally tall umbrella pines. This is also a good viewpoint towards the cross atop Ste-Victoire. Now, if you are doing Walk 35, *watch for your parking place*, 2km after passing above the château: pull over left to a bus shelter and a large sign of welcome to Vauvenargues. This is **Les Cabassols**, from where the GR9 climbs the mountain. Continuing west, soon Ste-Victoire disappears from view, but the road is edged with attractive fields.

Some 7km from Les Cabassols, turn sharp left on the D10f for BARRAGE DE BIMONT.

Through the pines you have a splendid view of the mountain and cross. There is a large parking area at the **Barrage de Bimont**★ (106km; crowded Sundays/ holidays). This huge reservoir, fed by the Canal de Provence, provides water for 22 communities around Aix and even supplements the supplies to Marseille. From the 100m/330ft-high dam there is a path to the summit of Ste-Victoire and a track to the Barrage Zola (Alternative walk 36-2); these are shown on the map on pages 128-129.

Leave the dam and turn right on the D10.

As you retrace your route on the north side of Ste-Victoire, you will have a fine view of its rippling flanks for the next 10 kilometres.

Beyond Vauvenargues and the D11 from the Montagne des Ubacs, keep right on the D10 for CLAPS.

Some 4km further on you pass below **La Citadelle** on the left, with its bright white limestone edge. Now the **Pic des Mouches** (1011m/3320ft), the highest summit on Ste-Victoire, rises on the right; beyond it, the mountain starts to tail off. There is limited parking at the **Col des Portes** (120.5km 📷), from where a path climbs to a *table d'orientation* on the Pic des Mouches. This is also a pleasant picnic area (⍽ a few hundred metres beyond the col), especially in spring, when blue grass lilies *(Aphyllanthes monspeliensis)* and white-flowering Montpellier *Cistus* bloom under the holly and holm oaks — but there is no view to Ste-Victoire from here. Entering Var, the road is numbered D223.

At a fork outside Le-Puits-de-Rians go right on the D23 for POURRIERES.

Notice the exceptionally slender, graceful trunks of the oaks here in the **Bois de Pourrières**. Some 4km along, limestone again makes its presence felt, bordering the road; then you round a bend and a fantastic edge rises before you — **Mont Aurélien** in the south, Ste-Victoire's little brother. Beautifully-coloured hedgerows take you into **Pourrières** (135.5km). Pity the poor village: its name signifies 'putrid', and supposedly recalls rotting corpses left on a battlefield here in 100BC.

Leave Pourrières on the D623 for PUYLOUBIER.

You travel across the plain shown on pages 4-5, where Ste-Victoire rises above a carpet of vineyards. This is a lovely run late in the afternoon, when the low sun highlights every nuance in the mountain's limestone ribs.

On crossing into **Bouches-du-Rhône** again, you come into **Puyloubier**, where the rose-coloured church with wrought-iron bell-cage sits nicely above the village.

From Puyloubier head west on the D17 for LE THOLONET.

Now on the **Route Cézanne★**, you skirt the southern foothills of

The Montagne Ste-Victoire from the D46 to Beaurecueil

The beautiful 18th-century château at Le Tholonet houses the offices of the Canal de Provence. This 220km-long watercourse, drawn principally from the Durance, has a total catchment network of 3000km and irrigates 115 communities in Bouches-du-Rhône and Var. Walk 36 would take you to an intriguing little gorge behind the château.

Ste-Victoire, a blaze of yellow- and blue-flowering blooms in spring. There are many pine-shaded parking places on this side of the mountain; all make fine picnic spots. The road passes to the right of **St-Antonin**, skirting the mountain in the setting shown on pages 126-127 (bottom). After you pass beneath the cross on Ste-Victoire (Croix de Provence), you curve downhill in hairpins. There are several routes up the mountain from this side, but they are all tougher than the ascents from the north.

On coming to **Le Tholonet** (158km), there is ample parking in front of the château shown above or in the plane-shaded square opposite. Walk 36 starts here and visits a pretty little reservoir southwest of the Lac de Bimont; engineered by Emile Zola's father 100 years before its post-war neighbour, it boasted the first arched dam in the world.

From Le Tholonet keep straight ahead on the D17, winding through pines and past impressive estates with wrought-iron gates. Just outside Aix you may glimpse the Château Noir on the right, where Cézanne spent several years at the turn of the 19th century. This road takes you straight into **Aix-en-Provence** (164km ✝M). Plan to spend a couple of days in this beautiful city, to visit the museums and spend the evenings strolling from fountain to fountain along the magnificent Cours Mirabeau, beneath the vaulting of plane trees. Then join the university students for an *apéritif* at one of the many outdoor cafés facing the elegant 17/18th-century mansions. One morning, head back east on the Route Cézanne to see the mountain in early light. Go past Le Tholonet and turn right on the D46 to Beaurecueil, from where you will have the splendid view shown on page 59.

✻ Walking

Those who go to France purely for a walking holiday are likely to be tackling the long linear GR routes. *This book has been written for motorists who want to tour the most beautiful roads and enjoy some glorious walks en route.* Very few of the walks are strenuous, and we don't include hikes to summits that can be reached by car (Utelle, for example). The walks have been chosen to highlight the great variety of landscapes in Provence and to focus on our favourite beauty spots.

Although the walks are scattered between the Alps and Aix, you should find many within easy reach (no more than an hour away by car or public transport) no matter where you are based. If you are staying in one area for a couple of weeks, visit the nearest *syndicat d'initiative* (tourist office) to get information about local walks and up-to-date **bus and train timetables** (many of our walks are accessible by public transport; see 'How to get there' at the top of the relevant page and transport information on the touring map).

Weather
Many walks in this book may be done the year round, but from mid-June to mid-September it will be far too hot to enjoy any but the easiest rambles. *Moreover, areas prone to forest fires (the Esterel, Maures and Ste-Victoire for example) may be closed to visitors from mid-July until mid-September.* Spring and autumn are the best seasons for walking; not only are the temperatures moderate, but there is an extravaganza of wild flowers and seasonal foliage. On the other hand, you will have to put up with a few days of torrential rain. In winter the walks in the Mercantour will be 'off bounds', and it may be *bitterly* cold atop Ste-Victoire or in the Verdon, even if there is no snow. *Always take local advice before walking in the high mountains between October and May.* The notorious *mistral* blows for about a third of the year (usually in winter and spring and usually for a *minimum* of three days). Often it is difficult to stand upright, and no walks should be attempted in areas exposed to this northerly wind.

What to take
No special equipment is needed for any of the walks, but proper **walking boots** are preferable to any other footwear. Most walks in Provence cross very stony terrain at some stage, and good ankle support is essential. In wet weather you

will also be glad of the waterproofing. A **sunhat** and high-protection **suncream** are equally important; there is a real risk of sunstroke on some walks. Each member of the party should carry a small rucksack, so that the chore of lugging the essentials is shared. *All year round* it is advisable to carry a first-aid kit, whistle, torch, spare socks and bootlaces, and some warm clothing (the *mistral* can blow up suddenly, with temperatures dropping up to 10°C/20°F!). A long-sleeved shirt and long trousers should be worn or carried, for sun protection and for making your way through the prickly plants of the *maquis*. Depending on the season, you may also need an anorak, light-weight rainwear, woollies and gloves. Optional items include swimwear, a Swiss Army knife, plastic cups and flasks, insect repellent. Mineral water is sold almost everywhere in plastic half-litre bottles; *it is imperative that each walker carries at least a half-litre of water — a full litre in hot weather.*

N uisances
We have never been bothered by dogs but, for peace of mind, you might like to invest in an ultrasonic **dog** deterrent: contact Sunflower Books, who sell them. Any snakes you may spot slithering out of your way will probably be harmless, but **vipers** (recognisable by the distinct triangular shape of the head) *do* exist (another good reason always to wear boots and long trousers). Take care if you move a log or stone, and *always* keep a look-out near drystone walls. Outside winter you may be plagued by an encyclopaedic array of **biting insects** — just when you are panting up a mountain or tucking into lunch. You may also encounter **beehives** along some of the routes; bees are not a problem if you keep your distance.

W aymarking, grading, safety
You will encounter **waymarking** on almost all the walks, but this is not necessarily helpful. Many routes have been waymarked over the years with different colours and symbols. Only the GR (Grande Randonnée) waymarking is meticulously maintained. Local councils change PR (Petite Randonnée) routes from year to year, often *without* removing old waymarks.*
Moreover, *our walks do not always follow the waymarked routes*. At the top of each walk we mention the waymarking colours *at time of writing;* although *most* PR waymarking is now yellow, this is not universal, and sometimes councils change the

---

*For this reason *never* follow local footpath waymarks without the corresponding *up-to-date* IGN map or details from the tourist office (you may have to buy a book from them). You could find yourself on a dangerous path that has not been maintained for years. Beware, too, of any walks described as *sportif*: they are always potentially hazardous.

colours for no apparent reason. Do, however, note these waymarking features, common to both PR and GR routes:

— A *flash* (stripe of paint) or *dot* (stipple of paint) indicates 'Route continues this way'. (The GR uses *two separate* flashes, red and white, and this must *never* be confused with a red flash on a white paint background, which is forestry marking, *not* route marking.)
— A right- or left-angled flash (or an arrow) means 'Change of direction'.
— An X means 'Wrong way'.

The walks have been **graded** for the deskbound person who nevertheless keeps reasonably fit. Our timings average 4km per hour on the flat, plus 20 minutes for every 100m/300ft of ascent. None of the walks ascends more than about 600m/2000ft. *Do* check your timings against ours on a short walk before tackling one of the longer hikes. Remember that these are *neat walking times;* increase the overall time by at least one-third, to allow for lunch breaks and nature-watching.

Safety depends in great part on *knowing what to expect and being properly equipped*. For this reason we urge you to read through the *whole* walk description at your leisure *before* setting out, so that you have a mental picture of each stage of the route and the landmarks. On *most* of our walks you will encounter other people — an advantage if you get into difficulty. Nevertheless, we advise you **never** to walk alone.

Maps

The **maps** in this book, adapted from the latest IGN 1:25,000 maps, have been reproduced at a scale of 1:50,000 or larger. All the latest IGN maps (the 'Top 25' Series) show many local and long-distance walks. Older IGN maps ('Série Bleue) show *only* GR routes *or none at all:* it is very difficult to plan a short or circular walk using these maps, because they do not indicate permissive routes; 'on the ground' you may come up against barbed wire or a new housing estate. If Top 25 maps are not available, you will have to seek out up-to-date walks from the local tourist office (see Bibliography).

Below is a key to the symbols on our walking maps.

motorway	spring, tank, etc	bus stop
main road	aqueduct	car parking
secondary road	church.chapel	railway station or tourist 'train'
minor road	shrine or cross	
motorable track	cemetery	castle, fort.ruins
other track	picnic tables	specified building
cart track, path, trail	pylon, wires	quarry, mine.cave
main walk	electricity wires	windmill.stadium
alternative walk	tourist office	walkers' signposts
watercourse, pipe	mill	monument, tower
height in metres	rock formation	campsite
	best views	antiquity

Walk 1: ON THE ROOFTOPS OF NICE

Distance: about 8km/5mi; 3h
Grade: Quite easy, with little ascent; descents (mostly on steps) of about 300m/1000ft overall. *Some signposting. IGN map 3742 OT*
Equipment: stout shoes will suffice. *NB:* Take a plan of Nice and information about the Colline du Château (from the tourist office). *No* refreshments available until you return to the port
How to get there: town 🚌 14 to the Mont Boron bus terminus
Short walk: Mont Boron and Mont Alban. 4km/2.5mi; 1h 15min. Easy. Follow the main walk to the 1h15min-point, then take 🚌 14 back to the centre.

Dipping your toes into a Cote d'Azur walking holiday couldn't be easier — you can start in the city of Nice, by strolling round three mini-mountains with beautiful woodlands and gardens, ancient remains and breathtaking views.

Start the walk at the BUS SHELTER on **Mont Boron**. Walk to the AREA MAP at the far side of the square. Two paths face you here: take the tarred footpath to the left, the **Sentier du Cap de Nice**. This circles Mont Boron below the old fort, at first giving the fine views shown opposite. Olive trees, holm oaks and pines shade the path-side benches. Soon views open out over Cap Ferrat (Walk 4) and its lighthouse. When you come to a road, the path continues just to the left of it (but first you might like to cross the road, to another fine viewpoint). When you reach a barrier, you are just 100m/yds short of your starting point (but it cannot be seen from here). Now take the trail that goes off left at a 90° angle, and walk round another barrier. This trail (**Circuit de Bellevue**) rounds the seaward side of the fort, circling the hill at a higher level. When this second circuit is complete, go left on the road and follow it in a curve to the right, back to the square with the bus shelter (**35min**).

Continue along the road past the AREA MAP, following signs for AUBERGE DE LA JEUNESSE. When the road curves right, take a tarred path off left (*ignore* the Allée du Bois Dormant just to the left of it). Rejoin the road and continue left uphill, quickly passing the MAISON FORESTIERE on the left. At

a Y-fork go right for FORT DU MT ALBAN, then cut a bend off the road by walking left through a picnic area. In early spring this road is a blaze of yellow-flowering tree-spurge (*Euphorbia dendroides*). From the **Fort du Mont Alban** (**55min**) the views down over Villefranche and its bay are superb.

Return the same way to the AREA MAP in the square on Mont Boron (**1h15min**). Now descend the concreted steps on the right (the **Chemin des Crêtes**). Keep straight downhill through mixed woodlands, accompanied by wrens and robins, crossing straight over roads. In 10 minutes you pass to the right of the richly-decorated **Notre-Dame du Perpétuel Secours**. When you reach the Boulevard Carnot/N98 *cross carefully (blind corners)*. The path continues just at the left side of the Hotel Marbella, heading towards the port and the Colline du Château. Make your way to the **Club Nautique** (🚌 20) and continue along the lovely residential stretch of the Boulevard Franck Pilatte. Follow the road inland (signposted 'Gare'), but turn left after about 20m/yds and walk to the PORT. Circle the port on the quays, then turn left towards the Promenade des Anglais, quickly coming to the beautiful MEMORIAL to the dead of World Wars I and II on

From Mont Boron: the Colline du Château with its arched war memorial punctuates the coast between the port and the Promenade des Anglais.

the right, its high arch carved into the **Colline du Château (2h)**. Keep rounding the hill, until you come to the lift (ASCENSEUR), and pay the small fee to ride up to the top (or climb the adjacent steps 90m/300ft). Allow a good half hour to potter about the top of the hill — not missing the Tour Bellanda, the mosaics, the ruins of two cathedrals (10-12C and 14C) which once stood in the grounds of the Duke of Savoy's château, the beautiful waterfall fed by the

Vésubie … and the views!
To return to town you *could* take the lift or adjacent steps or pick up the tourist train. We usually walk down via the cemeteries: take the steps below the waterfall, down to a road. Turn right, then take steps on the left signposted CIMETIERES, VIELLE VILLE. From the lowest (Catholic) cemetery, take the road downhill to the right, then make a sharp hairpin bend to the left on Montée Eberlé. This leads to the **Place Garibaldi (3h)**.

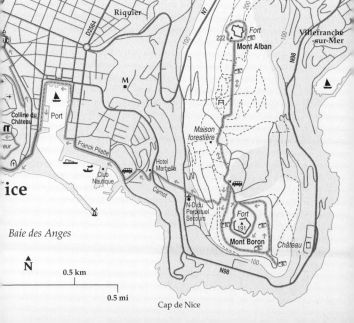

Walk 2: MONT CHAUVE D'ASPREMONT

Distance: 10.5km/6.5mi; 3h20min
Grade: moderate ascent of 345m/
1130ft and descent of 530m/
1740ft. Good, but stony, paths
and tracks underfoot. Little shade.
Red and white GR, yellow PR
waymarking. *IGN map 3742 OT*
Equipment: see page 61; refreshments available at Aspremont
How to get there: 🚌 to Aspremont; return on Nice town 🚌 25
or 70 to the centre
**Alternative walk: Aspremont —
Mont Chauve d'Aspremont —
Aspremont.** 8km/5mi; 2h40min.
Grade as main walk (ascent/
descent of 345m/1130ft). Follow
the main walk to the FORT (1h
25min). The return path to Aspremont leaves from the north side of
the outer wall (yellow waymark on
the protective railing). *Watch
carefully for the yellow waymarks* on
this narrow goats' path which
descends through broom, lavender
and thyme, heading towards the

houses of Sambule below. At a
wide crossing path, turn right,
then keep downhill until you come
to a TUNNEL on the left
(30 minutes from the fort). Walk
through it (no torch needed) and
exit looking straight across to the
neighbouring (ruined) fort,
Tourrette. Head right on a gravel
track and turn left on another track
after 200m/yds. At the Y-fork that
follows almost immediately, bear
left. When you come to a yellow
arrow pointing up to the right,
ignore it; keep ahead on the lovely
grassy path, now making straight
for Aspremont. Keep left again at
the next Y-fork. Some 500m/yds
further on, the path deteriorates
and zigzags downhill over skiddy
rubble. When you meet a cart
track, turn left. On coming to a
lane (**Chemin de la Bergerie**),
follow it to the left. This takes you
back to the GR51, which you
follow back to Aspremont.

T he flanks of Mont Chauve ('Bald Mountain') are virtually
treeless, so all along this invigorating ridge walk you'll
have unimpeded views. The sense of isolation is wonderful,
too; it's hard to believe you're at the edge of the Riviera —
until you take in the panorama from the massive fort!

Start out at the BUS STOP/CAR PARK
in **Aspremont**. Walk towards NICE
on the D14, but quickly turn right
down the **Chemin de la Vallière**
(GR waymarks), taking concrete
steps down into the **Magnan**

Valley. Meet the D14 again in five
minutes and go straight over, up a
lane. In two minutes keep ahead
on a stony path. At a PYLON
(**10min**), turn sharp right uphill
on the GR5. (The path straight

View north from the flanks of Mont Chauve d'Aspremont

ahead is the GR51, return route for the Alternative walk.) Rising on this stony path, you enjoy a fine view back over Aspremont on its conical hill and to the perched villages of Le Broc and Carros on the far side of the Var. Soon you pass a ruined building, **Fondalin** (**25min**) in a very pleasant, grassy setting. The path rises gently through golden grasses and *garrigues* until, when you are above Nice's crematorium on the main road, the sea comes into view ahead.

Les Faces (**35min**) is the next little ruin on route. Rising below abandoned hillside terracing, you come to a final ruin (**Les Templiers**; **50min**) and reach a fork 200m/yds further on. Leave the GR here: turn sharp left uphill on a cart track, now following yellow waymarks and enjoying some fine views down over Nice and the coast. On approaching a rock face, follow the track in a U-bend to the left and then a sharp turn to the right (where a track goes straight ahead back towards Les Faces). The observatory on Mont Gros, as well as Mont Alban, Mont Boron and the port (Walk 1) provide focal points on this stretch. The track contours above the rock face, with a fine view to the right along the Crête de Graus — the ridge you will follow back to Nice. On meeting a road (**Piste des Morgues**; **1h05min**), follow it uphill in tight hairpin bends to the SUMMIT of **Mont Chauve d'Aspremont** (**1h25min**). The massive old FORT here, the last in a line of coastal defenses stretching from Ste-Agnès (Walk 9) to Nice, is one of the best viewpoints on the Côte d'Azur. While the coastal views are mesmerising, don't forget to look back north — up towards the Mercantour and the Alps! Take time, too, to walk down around the grassy 'moat' between the inner and outer walls.

From the fort retrace your steps to the GR5 (**2h05min**). Now follow it to the left along the **Crête de Graus**. A slight rise takes you up to a COL in about 35 minutes; ignore any minor or crossing paths, keep heading along the main path, towards a PYLON. The path descends to the ruined walls of the **Château Reynard** (**2h55min**), from where there is another fine view. As the descent becomes more pronounced, you come to a T junction: go left, towards another PYLON. At the pylon, *ignore* the yellow PR route straight ahead; go right on the GR, down towards a field. In the field, go left on a crossing path, into the olive groves and pines of a picnic area with tables (**Aire St-Michel**; **3h12min**). On meeting a lane, follow it downhill past villas, to a BUS SHELTER on **Avenue Jules Roman** (**3h20min**).

Walk 3: PEILLE AND PEILLON

Distance: 11.5km/7.1mi; 3h35min
Grade: moderate ascents/descents of about 500m/1640ft overall. Little shade on the outgoing path; plenty of shade on the return. Good yellow PR waymarking around Peillon; poor waymarking around Peille. *IGN map 3742 OT*
Equipment: see page 61; walking stick. Refreshments available at Peille and Peillon
How to get there: 🚌 to Peillon.

Peille is served by bus, but there is not ample time for the circuit.
Alternative routes: Peillon council has waymarked the **Circuit de Lourquière** and the **path from Peillon to La Grave**. If you are travelling by public transport you could take a 🚌 to Peille, do the walk *in reverse* (via the St-Pancrace Chapel and the Galambert Stream) to Peillon, then descend to La Grave (🚌, 🚐).

O ld trails — some dating from Roman times — are followed in this circuit via the exquisite perched villages of Peille and Peillon. Which will you prefer? Purely from a waymarking point of view, it has to be Peillon!

Start out at the 18th-century FOUNTAIN in **Peillon**. Walk up the paved steps behind it, then turn left (↑: PEILLE VILLAGE 2H). You pass an IRON CROSS and come into olive groves, with the **Lourquière** mountain rising on the right. At a first fork, keep ahead (↑: PEILLE VILLAGE) and at the next go right (same ↑). There is a beautiful view back to the thimble-like spur of Peillon now, and the path enters a gorge. When a METAL GATE blocks the path (**10min**), turn *sharp left* uphill. Eventually the old stone-laid trail passes below the red-hued climbing rocks of the **Baus Roux**, then crosses the **Galambert Stream** on a FIRST STONE BRIDGE (**30min**). Four minutes later, ignore a path forking back to the right; keep ahead. Ignore another path off right and keep ahead over a SECOND STONE BRIDGE (**40min**; ↑: CHAPELLE ST-PANCRACE, PEILLE). Continue uphill, straight towards the masts on the Cime de la Morgelle (but this 1076m-high peak rises well to the east of your ongoing route).
Tar comes underfoot in **Buampin** (**50min**): keep uphill until the road curves right, then walk straight ahead alongside the fence of a BUILDERS' YARD on your left.

At a fork 20m/yds along, keep right; continue across a driveway and up to the D53 (**1h**). Follow the road to the left for 200m/yds and, at the junction with the D22, turn sharp right. Walk up the D22 for 150m/yds, then turn hard back left on a path (CAIRN). This pretty path passes the ruined **Chapelle St-Pancrace**, then descends gently through pines, back to the D53. Follow the road to the right. When the road bends right, by a rock promontory on the left (**1h25min**), your on-going path dives down left just *before* the rock promontory. *Note: this path is badly eroded, with unprotected drops to the left; you will get to Peille almost as quickly by continuing along the D53 — a safer option.*
The path (or the road) gives you some superb views of Peille's pride and joy: its well-engineered *Via Ferrata* — climbing walls with iron hand-holds and suspension bridges over the dramatic **Farquin Gorge**. After crossing a stone bridge, the path rises to the MUSEUM at Peille (**1h45min**). Once you have wandered around this beautifully-sited village strung out along the ravine walls, make your way to the round tower of the HOTEL DE VILLE and descend

the adjacent steps (**Rue des Pous**). Keep zigzagging almost due south for about 10 minutes, until you reach the FINAL HAIPIN BEND OF THE D53 below Peille, where your ongoing path descends concrete steps at the left (yellow and blue paint waymarks; **2h**). At a fork reached very quickly, take the descending path to the right (with a water pipe on your left). Keep downhill across traces of hunters' paths, passing to the left of some houses in 10 minutes and crossing the **Farquin Stream** on a LOG BRIDGE five minutes later (**2h15min**).

From here follow the notes carefully; it is easy to get lost in these beautiful, dense oak woods, as all the paths are waymarked in yellow! Rise up from the bridge, in five minutes ignoring a path back to the right. Pass to the left of a huge boulder which bears some yellow and red waymarks. Ten minutes up from the bridge, ignore a large cairn on the right but, three minutes later, another TALL CAIRN marks an *important junction, where you must turn sharp left.* (The path straight ahead eventually joins a

Peillon on Christmas Day

track, then descends to Paravielle and La Grave de Peille.) *Two minutes later, at a Y-fork, keep right.* In 10 minutes the path curls round to the right at the foot of a very large SCREE (**2h40min**). *If you have not reached this point within 30 minutes from the log bridge, you have gone wrong.* Ten minutes later the path runs through pines and tall grass higher up the ridge — a very attractive setting. You pass to the left of a BUILDING (**2h55min**), then curl left towards the crests. As you push through masses of broom *(this stretch can be very overgrown in spring)*, there are some open views down right to the huge quarry at La Grave. Rise to a COL AND MARKER STONE 128 on the right (**3h05min**); keep straight ahead here, ignoring a path back to the right. Seven minutes later, at a Y-fork, keep right, quickly passing to the right of a CAIRN. From here the path descends gently, eventually coming to a fork: keep straight ahead (🌂: PEILLON VILLAGE). A stone-laid trail takes you to the next fork, where you go right (same 🌂). At a third fork, keep straight on, retracing your steps past the IRON CROSS to the FOUNTAIN in **Peillon** (**3h35min**). Before leaving, be sure to visit the **Chapelle des Pénitents Blancs** with its Renaissance frescoes.

Walk 4: AROUND CAP FERRAT

Distance: 8km/5mi; 2h45min
Grade: easy, with ups and downs of about 130m/425ft. Adequate shade. *No* waymarks, but easily followed. *IGN map 3742 OT*
Equipment: see page 61; swimming things. Refreshments available at St-Jean-Cap-Ferrat
How to get there: 🚆 or 🚌 to St-Jean-Cap-Ferrat
Short walk: Pointe de St-Hospice. 2.8km/1.7mi; 1h10min; easy). Follow the main walk to the 1h-point, then return to the port.
Alternative walk: Beaulieu — Cap Ferrat — Beaulieu. 13km/

8mi; 3h55min. Grade as main walk. Access: 🚆, 🚌 or 🚤 to Beaulieu. However you travel, make your way down to the casino and marina, from where a seafront walkway (**Promenade Maurice-Rouvier**) runs south along the coast to St-Jean-Cap-Ferrat. After completing the main walk, return the same way to Beaulieu.
Note: When you meet the D125 near the end of the walk, you can first turn *left,* to visit the Éphrussi de Rothschild Foundation, with its beautiful gardens and Ile de France Museum (paid entrance).

Lovely any time of year, this walk is especially enjoyable on a bright and bracing winter's day. You'll walk below the exotic gardens of some of the most exquisite properties on the Riviera, with far-reaching views out to sea and for miles east and west along the 'Azure Coast'.

Begin the walk overlooking the PORT at **St-Jean-Cap-Ferrat**. Walk south, then east, round the port, then go up AVENUE JEAN MERMOZ, keeping the Voile d'Or restaurant on your left. Take steps on the left down to the Paloma Beach restaurant. Here you pick up a coastal walkway running round the **Pointe de St-Hospice**, with fine views over to Eze, La Turbie, the Tête de Chien, Monaco and Cap Martin. After rounding the point, take steps on the right (⌐) up to the 19th-century **Chapelle**

St-Hospice with its huge bronze-painted statue of Virgin and Child. An 18th-century TOWER is adjacent, but is on private land and not fully visible.
Then return to the coastal path and turn right. Beyond the **Pointe du Colombier**, the path enters a lovely pine wood at the edge of a little bay (**Les Fossettes**), then meets a road at a T-junction (**1h**). Turn left here. *(But for the Short walk, turn right, and retrace your outgoing route back to the port.)* Follow the road past the next little bay, **Les Fosses**.

Approaching the harbour at St-Jean-Cap-Ferrat on the seafront promenade from Beaulieu, with the Pointe de St-Hospice in the background

At the next T-junction, eight minutes later, go left and walk round a metal barrier. You pick up the coastal walkway again and begin to round **Cap Ferrat**. Trailing superb views inland (and dodging the sea-spray), now you can really stride out, while watching the yachts and high-speed ferries sailing to and from the nearby ports of Villefranche and Nice.

The path passes above many pretty little inlets, and below the LIGHT-HOUSE (**1h30min**; paid entrance, if you decide to climb up to it). The path ends at the **Plage de Passable** (**2h30min**). Climb the steps at the left of the beach restaurant, cross straight over a road and go up more steps. At the next road, walk left for 160m/yds, then go right, up an alley. You emerge on the main D125 (**Avenue Denis Séméria**); the TOURIST OFFICE is on your left and a BUS STOP is opposite. Turn right and, at a Y-fork, keep left on Avenue Séméria. At the next Y-fork go left. Keep following Avenue Séméria against the one-way traffic system all the way back to the PORT at **St-Jean**. A BUS STOP is opposite the MAIRIE (**2h45min**).

Rounding the east side of the cape, with St-Hospice opposite and the Tête de Chien rising in the distance. Above: the lighthouse, one of the most modern in France

Walk 5: RAVIN DU MAL INFERNET

See map pages 74-75
Distance: 7.5km/4.7mi; 1h55min
Grade: easy, with an ascent of
under 100m/330ft near the end of
the walk. However, the tracks and
paths are stony underfoot, and
there is almost no shade. Red and
white GR waymarking. *IGN map
3544 ET*
Equipment: see page 61; swimming things. No refreshments
available beyond Agay
How to get there: ⛙ to the
parking area at the Col de Belle-
Barbe, just north of Agay (Car
tour 1)

**Alternative walk: Sommet des
Grosses Grues and Balcons de la
Côte d'Azur.** 18km/11.2mi;
about 7h; moderate-strenuous,
with ascents/descents of about
550m/1800ft overall. Access as
main walk. Follow the main walk
to the Lac de l'Ecureuil (55min),
then continue on the GR51 to the
Col Notre-Dame and the Sommet
des Grosses Grues. Return the
same way — or, from the Col
Notre-Dame, vary the return (see
purple lines on the map). Tremendous coastal views throughout;
carry *plenty of food and water*.

T he crystalline Esterel is as old as the Maures (see page 50).
You don't have to be a geologist to marvel at the colours
of these porphyry rocks, with a wealth of minerals sparkling
in rainbow hues. The ideal time to visit is early spring, when
the streams are full and the hillsides aglow with flowers.

Start out at the **Col de Belle-
Barbe**. Walk behind the barrier
(🛈: *RESERVE BIOLOGIQUE DU MAL
INFERNET*) and follow the earthen
track; the dramatic outline of the
Pic de l'Ours is straight ahead.
Beyond a small lake, the boulder-
strewn **Ravin du Grenouillet**
opens up on your right. When you
come to an old parking area,
continue downhill to the left on
the stony track, to cross the bed of
the **Mal Infernet Stream** on a
concrete FORD (Gué on the map;
15min). Just past here, ignore a
wide path off to the right (to the
Rocher du Gravier). As you round
a bend, the Ravin du Mal Infernet
reveals its tortured landscape:
jagged red rocks rise on both sides
of the limpid stream.
Just after passing a SPRING on the
right (**30min**), you reach one of
the prettiest settings on the walk:
the stream is dammed to form a
glassy pool, which spills over into
a lovely waterfall. Soon the banks
slope gently down to the stream
— an ideal spot for a swim or
picnic. Two-three minutes later

the GR51 climbs up left to the Col
Aubert; this will be our return
route. Keeping ahead, in another
five minutes the gorge curls round
and you look straight ahead to the
Mamelon de l'Ecureuil, a high
rounded hill. A few holm and cork
oaks provide welcome shade.
At a fork, turn left downhill and
cross a BRIDGE (**50min**). The Pic
de l'Ours, with its fractured
crown, rises on the right here, as
you continue into a dramatic
'wild-west' setting. Soon the
sound of rushing water heralds
your approach to the tiny **Lac de
l'Ecureuil** (Squirrel Lake;
55min), another lovely picnic
spot. Several other waymarked
trails continue north and east from
here; see the Alternative walk or
refer to IGN map 3544 ET.
Return from the lake to where the
GR leaves the track (**1h10min**).
Cross the river on the metal mesh
bridge and follow the stony
footpath up the far side, climbing
quickly, with beautiful views down
over the stream. Accompanied by
butterflies galore, climb to the **Col**

The Ravin du Mal Infernet (above),
view across the Ravin des Lentisqus to
the Pic du Cap Roux and Le St-Pilon
(middle), the Mal Infernet (below)

Aubert (**1h25min**), where the
GR goes right up to the Col du
Baladou. Leave the GR here: go
left along a flat stretch of shadeless
path. Watch out now for the
stunted strawberry trees (*Arbutus
unedo*) with their unmistakeable
red fruits — which are edible but
quite sour. Ignore the path off to
the right just below the **Pic du
Baladou**; continue to the left.
From the highest point in this
climb there is a fine view across
the Ravin des Lentisques to the
twin summits of Cap Roux, rising
above a bib of trees. The Pic du
Cap Roux (453m) is on the left;
Le St-Pilon (445m; not within our
map area) on the right.
Now the wide stony path
descends, with a good view over
your outgoing track and the
stream bed down on the left. The
green basins and red rock folds of
the Esterel rise all around you.
Notice the pale olive-green porphyry rock underfoot along here.
The Pic du Baladou path comes in
from the right (**1h55min**), and in
a trice you are back at the **Col de
Belle-Barbe**.

Walk 6: CIRCUIT ABOVE THEOULE-SUR-MER

Distance: 8km/5mi; 2h10min from Théoule centre; 12km/7.4mi; 3h30min from Théoule's railway station

Grade: easy, with an ascent/descent of 130m/425ft overall. Some of the tracks and paths are stony underfoot; little shade. Red and white GR, yellow PR way-marking. *IGN map 3544 ET*

Equipment: see page 61; swimming things. Refreshments available at Théoule-sur-Mer

How to get there: 🚆, 🚌 or 🚗 (Car tour 1) to Théoule-sur-Mer (but see 'Distance' above)

One of the advantages of a break — even a weekend — on the Côte d'Azur is the excellent public transport. There's a good week's walking in this book for which you won't need a hire car — especially if you're based between Cannes and Nice. This little gem is a perfect example but, by referring to the paths on the map highlighted in purple (all waymarked), you can make up any combination of routes. We like to do this walk by train, but you can also return by bus from the beachside restaurant at the end of the walk.

Our walk begins at Théoule's *RAILWAY STATION*, 1km north of the village on the N98. While you *can* just follow the N98 south to Théoule from here, it's preferable to follow the GR51 signs from the station. The GR crosses the railway line 400m/yds south of the station and runs through a little valley, before returning to the N98 and coming into **Théoule-sur-Mer (40min)**. Turn right off the N98 at signs for *MAIRIE/POSTE*. Pass both (on your left) and keep straight ahead. When this street makes a hairpin turn to the left (back to the N98), continue ahead on a track (■: *COL DE THEOULE*), rising above the railway line, into the Esterel.

Just as the railway enters the **Tunnel des Saumes (1h10min)**, be sure to turn off right, following the GR along a footpath below the track. This path then rises to the **Col de Théoule (1h30min)**, a major crossroads. From the col, head southwest on a *footpath* between two tracks (■: *ESQUILLON*). The path heads straight towards the Pointe de l'Esquillon, eventually widening into a track. When you come to a road junction some

40m/130ft above the N98 (**2h**), turn left on a 'balcony' footpath and walk northeast, with fine coastal views, eventually passing above Port-la-Galère.

At a fork, keep right, continuing northeast above the N98 on a lane (you will pass a *CHAPEL* on the right). As you approach the **Pointe de l'Aiguille** (where a *PARK* is up to the left; **2h35min**), cross over the N98 and go down

In February mimosas brighten the balcony path above the coast

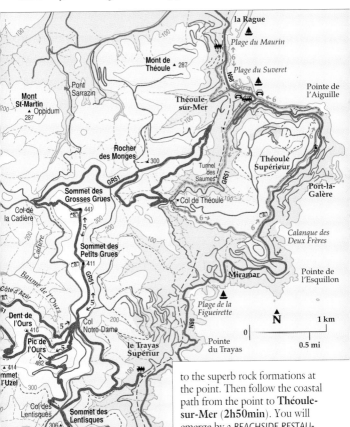

to the superb rock formations at the point. Then follow the coastal path from the point to **Théoule-sur-Mer** (**2h50min**). You will emerge by a *BEACHSIDE RESTAU-RANT (BUS SHELTER)*. From here retrace your outgoing route back to the *STATION* (**3h30min**).

Walk 7: CAP DU DRAMONT

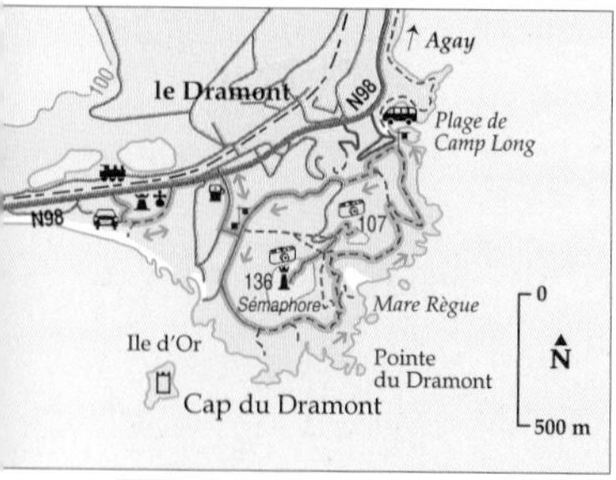

Distance: 5.5km/3.4mi; 2h
Grade: fairly easy ascents/descents of about 200m/650ft overall, but you must be sure-footed. Some signposting. *IGN map 3544 ET*
Equipment: see page 61; swimming things. Refreshments available at Camp Long
How to get there: 🚗 or 🚂 to Cap du Dramont; one can also return by 🚌 from Camp Long

With the exception of Le Trayas, Dramont's red porphry rock *calanques* are the most beautiful on the coast. When the sun sparkles on the azure sea through the shimmering pines, this landscape is unbelieveably beautiful.

Start out at the LE DRAMONT RAILWAY STATION: cross the N98 to the monument commemorating the landing of the US Army's 36th Division on 15 August 1944 (car parking), then walk east towards Agay. Just past the petrol station, turn right on the Boulevard du Sémaphore. After some 300m/yds, turn left at house No 245 (**Le Haut du Poussaï**), quickly coming to a FORESTRY HOUSE (⚑ with a 'trident' symbol, showing the Dramont circuits).

Walking in an anti-clockwise direction, the square tower on the **Ile d'Or** quickly becomes a focal point. Take a break on the red rocks at the **Pointe du Dramont**, before rising above the largest of the coves, the **Mare Règue**. Turn left up a path here, to a PASS between the two highest 'peaks' on the cape.

First turn left to visit the **Sémaphore** (with viewpoint; **50min**); then return to the pass and walk up to the **Belvédère de la Batterie**. Both are superb viewpoints down over the deeply-etched coves, southwest to the Golfe de Fréjus and the Maures, and northeast to the Esterel and the Golfe de Napoule.

Return to the circuit path and continue to the **Plage de Camp Long** (**1h35min**; BUS STOP), where you can take a break at the beachside RESTAURANT.

The main walk returns from here to the BARRIER (⚑) on the south side of the beach, from where you follow the path on the northern side of the cape, back past the FORESTRY HOUSE, to the STATION (**2h**). But if you came by train, you could instead follow the concreted coastal path from here to Agay (also **2h**) and catch the train there. (This path runs — with some interruptions — all the way to Antibes; we take in part of it at Théoule, on Walk 6.)

View east from the Cap du Dramont, to the Pointe de Baumette and the Pic du Cap Roux

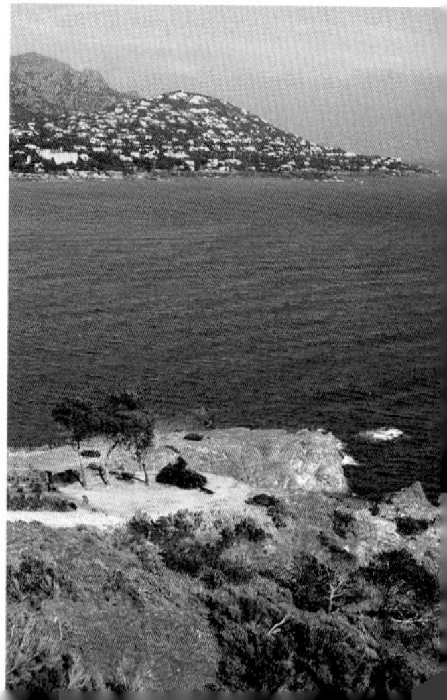

Walk 8: FROM LA TURBIE TO EZE-BORD-DE-MER

Distance: 8km/5mi; 3h15min
Grade: easy ascent of 155m/510ft, but strenuous descent of 600m/1970ft. Little shade. Yellow PR waymarking. *IGN map 3742 OT*
Equipment: see page 61; walking stick(s). Refreshments available at La Turbie and Eze
How to get there: 🚌 to La Turbie; return by 🚌 or 🚋 from Eze-Bord-de-Mer
Shorter walk: La Turbie — Eze Village. 6km/3.7mi; 2h20min. Fairly easy, but a steep descent of 280m/920ft. Follow the main walk to Eze Village and return by 🚌. This avoids the final 320m/

1050ft of descent. You may like to visit the exquisite Jardin Exotique at Eze.
Alternative walk: La Turbie — Maison de la Nature — La Turbie. 8km/5mi; 2h50min. Easy ascent/descent of 155m/510ft. 🚗 (Car tour 2) or 🚌 to La Turbie. Follow the main walk to the 1h40min-point, then continue along the corniche track, forking left to the **Cime de la Forna**. Descend from there back to the reservoirs and retrace your steps to La Turbie. (Optional detour: take in part of the **Sentier botanique**, with a *table d'orientation*).

O n this walk you will enjoy some of the finest views on the whole of the Riviera. The main walk rises gently along the north side of the Grande Corniche crest, with superb views up to the mountains, before crossing the shoulder — to a magnificent coastal panorama. From here the main walk dives south, with plunging views over Eze and Cap Ferrat, while the Alternative walk contours east along the old corniche military track, with coastal views towards Italy.

The walk begins at the MAIRIE in on the main road (D2564, the **Grande Corniche**) in **La Turbie**. Cross over the road to the Hotel Napoléon, then turn left. After 600m/yds, ignore the D2204 off right to the motorway; cross the wide junction and walk past a cylindrical PILLAR WITH AN IRON CROSS on the top and a builders'

merchants (both on the right). At the end of the builders' perimeter fence, turn right up the **Chemin de la Forna** (**10min**). There are fine views back to the Trophée des Alpes as you climb. As the concrete runs out, keep ahead on a cart track, to pass a RESERVOIR (**20min**). Just before a second, square reservoir, turn left up a

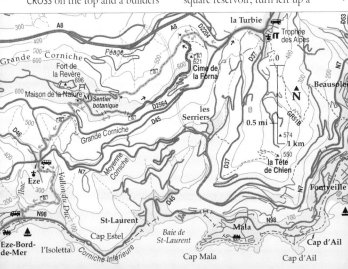

Eze Village

wide path, ignoring a lesser path straight ahead. In two minutes keep straight ahead (⌐: FORT DE LA REVERE). *(The Alternative walk returns via the 'Cime de la Forna' path to the left here.)*
Now a lovely path through tall grass takes you along the northern flanks of the **Grande Corniche**, just below the crest. You look north to Utelle, where the chapel shown on page 23 teeters on the edge of the cliff, and the mountains of the Mercantour. The Fort de la Revère crowns the rise to the east, above two forestry park buildings. From here the frenetic jockeying for position at the motorway toll booths below seems a world away.
On meeting the U-bend of a track, tun left uphill (⌐: FORT DE LA REVERE). You emerge at the **Maison de la Nature** (**1h25min**), with an interesting little museum, well-landscaped gardens, and picnic tables. Before continuing towards Eze, walk downhill to the coastal overlook (with benches) and follow the corniche track for short way. After five minutes, just before the FIRST TUNNEL, a **Sentier botanique** (with a *table d'orientation*) turns sharply up to the left — a possible detour. Continue as far as the SECOND TUNNEL (**1h 40min**), to take in the superb coastal panorama. *(The Alternative walk continues along this track towards La Turbie.)*
Retrace your steps to the Maison de la Nature and start walking up

the road towards the fort. But after less than 100m/yds, turn left down a footpath (⌐: EZE VILLAGE). This pretty path descends through tall grass above some luxurious villas. On coming to a concrete drive, follow it downhill to the right. Keep right, downhill, at further junctions, until you meet the **Grande Corniche** again (**2h05min**). Cross *carefully*, turn right for 20m/yds, then turn left down a lane, the **Chemin Serre de Forque**. The shade of pines is welcome here, but the descent is *very* steep. Keep straight down, whether by path, steps, or tar, until you meet the N7, the **Moyenne Corniche**, opposite the entrance to **Eze Village** (**2h20min**; BUS SHELTER, CAFES). Take a break here before, knees a-tremble, you begin the final descent.
Cross the road and head up into Eze, passing the TOURIST OFFICE on your right. Just past the **Frago-nard Perfumery** on your left, turn left down the **Chemin Frédéric Nietzche** (⌐: EZE MER). This wide old trail descends in gentle zigzags through a surprisingly wild valley (**Vallon du Duc**) above deeply-cut *calanques*. Eventually the path turns right, crosses a COL (**2h 50min**) and makes the final descent — with fine views over Cap Ferrat. When you meet the N98 (**Corniche Inférieure**), turn right to the BUS STOP. The RAILWAY STATION and TOURIST OFFICE are 400m/yds further along, on the south side of the road (**3h15min**).

Walk 9: FROM STE-AGNÈS TO CASTELLAR

Distance: 7km/4.3mi; 2h35min
Grade: easy-moderate ups and downs — about 500m/1640ft of descent overall and 270m/885ft of ascent (of which 200m is at the end of the walk). Red and white GR waymarking. *IGN map 3742 OT*
Equipment: see page 61; refreshments available at Ste-Agnès,

Monti and Castellar
How to get there: 🚌 to Ste-Agnès; return by bus from Castellar
Short walk: Ste-Agnès — Monti. 4.5km/2.8mi; 1h35min. Easy. Follow the walk to Monti and return by bus (avoids the final climb into Castellar).

The tangle of old cobbled lanes at Ste-Agnès, woven below arched passageways, is strongly evocative of medieval times. But although this 'highest of Europe's coastal villages' has always been strategically important (the fort was the most southerly defence of the Maginot Line), it wasn't accessible by road until 1933. This walk mostly follows the undulations of an old mule trail to Castellar — another perched village and, like St-Agnès, home to many artists and artisans.

The walk begins at the **Col St-Sébastien**, 200m/yds below **Ste-Agnès**, at the junction with the D22 to the Col de Gorbio. There's a medieval CHAPEL here, a FOUNTAIN, and a barrage of signposts. Follow the old cobbled footpath descending below the chapel, the GR51 (➚: LA VIRETTE, MONTI, CASTELLAR). In six minutes, when you have to go through an electrified wire fence, use the insulated handle to open the gate and close it behind you. As you descend into the wilderness of the **Borrigo Valley**, it's hard to believe that you're just a short way inland from the busy coast. You pass a stand of cypresses that once gave welcome shade to travellers ascending to Ste-Agnès and descend to the grassy banks of the stream, a lovely place to while away an hour … or three! When you come to the stream crossing,

the horses from the enclosure above may already be slaking their thirst. After a short rise up the far bank, another electrified fence sees you out of the horses' pastures. Look ahead now to your destination — the honey-hued buildings of Castellar, strung along a ridge.
You pass through a rock chaos in a grove of trees (obviously a popular shady picnic spot) and then another rock chaos. Beyond a small stream bed, you rise to the ruined hamlet of **La Virette** (**35min**). Descending steeply from the ruins, watch carefully for the GR 'change of direction' sign and turn *sharp left* downhill, *ignoring* any yellow waymarks. Cross another stream (in the **Ravin de Merthea**) and rise quite steeply, past a short narrow section with a drop to the right. As you head southeast on the far side of this ravine, look

back to Ste-Agnès, where its strategic position on the rocky escarpment is evident. Your eye will also be drawn to the motorway below, and the Monastère de l'Annonciade at Menton.

Dip into yet another little gulley, the **Ravin de Cabrolles** — a cool glen in summer, where ivy twines round the trees. Having climbed up the far side, a wide cobbled trail comes in from the left behind you; here you look straight down on Cap Martin (Walk 10). Straight away you come onto a newly-bulldozed track: follow it downhill to the right for 25m/yds, then turn sharp left in a U-bend, down a jeep track. At a Y-fork, keep right. As you descend towards Monti, ignore another track off to the right.

On coming to a concrete-surfaced T-junction, turn right. Steps take you down to the CHURCH at **Monti** (1h35min). Cross over to the BUS SHELTER; your concrete path continues just behind it (although it looks as if you are walking straight into someone's house!). Descend towards an industrial area but, just before reaching it, be sure to go straight ahead along a track (just past a huge pylon). Walk to the left of a breeze-block wall with glass on top (probably the local swimming pool).

Now you start to round the final large valley before Castellar, the **Torrent Careï**. Immediately after crossing a stream, keep left uphill at a Y-fork. Then, just as you start to rise on concrete steps, fork right on a path, through a pretty, wooded section. Cross another stream and, on meeting a concrete road, follow it uphill to the left. But a short way up, fork sharp right (⌐: CASTELLAR). This takes you down a concrete path. Cross the main stream and, at a fork, keep left uphill (⌐: CASTELLAR 1H). But fork right just 15 paces along.

The walk follows centuries-old cobbled mule trails.

As you rise you can look north to the Caramel Viaduct on the far side of the road to Sospel (see Car tour 2 and page 130). The path climbs in easy zigzags, sometimes through vineyards, and with an excellent view to Castellar on the approach. On coming to a crossing concrete lane, turn left uphill to a CHAPEL on the **Avenue St-Anton** in **Castellar** (2h35min). Follow the road uphill to the right, then take steps up right, into the heart of the village. At the top of the steps there is an IRON CROSS; opposite is the BUS STOP.

Castellar, like Sospel, is aglow with the warm, rich colours of nearby Italy.

Walk 10: CAP MARTIN

Distance: 5km/3mi; 1h45min
Grade: easy, with gentle ups and downs, mostly on a concrete walkway. *IGN map 3742 OT*
Equipment: see page 61; bathing things. Refreshments at Cabbé
How to get there: 🚒 or 🚌 to the Cabbé railway station (or 🚐 to Cabbé, but the N7 is 80m/260ft above the station, so allow extra time for the descent and climb back up)
Note: You could begin by visiting Roquebrune (🚐) and then walk 250m/820ft down to the coast.

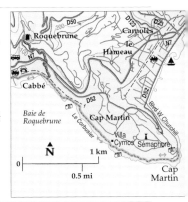

C ap-Martin is to Menton what Cap Ferrat is to Nice — both exclusive enclaves of the seriously wealthy. But their coastal paths are accessible to everyone, so for a while you can be 'master of all you survey' — the princely views are free.

Start the walk at the **Cabbé** RAILWAY STATION. Cross the bridge over the railway, then turn left and make your way over to the coastal path, **Le Corbusier** (**5min**). Trailing fine views back to Monaco, you pass several spurs down to jumping-off points where you could swim but, remember, the sea is at least 10m/30ft deep here. (The path is named in memory of the architect, who drowned while swimming off these rocks.)
You pass below the **Villa Cyrnos**, once the home of the Emperess Eugénie, where Winston Churchill came to dine and paint. Finally you pass the grounds of the exclusive Résidence du Cap hotel, then round the tip of the cape, with fine views over to Menton. The path ends at the **Boulevard Winston Churchill** (**55min**). Retrace your steps from here. With views focussing on Monaco, Cap Ferrat, the Tête de Chien, La Turbie and the perched village of Roquebrune, return to the **Cabbé** RAILWAY STATION (**1h45min**).

Top: pathside loggia; below: view to Menton and the peaks east of Sospel

Walk 11: ABOVE SOSPEL

See also photograph pages 14-15
Distance: 9km/5.6mi; 3h
Grade: moderate, with ascents/descents of 430m/1410ft overall. Red and white GR, yellow PR waymarking. *IGN map 3741 ET*
Equipment: see page 61; refreshments available at Sospel
How to get there: 🚌 (Car tour 2) or 🚍 or 🚗 to Sospel
Short walk: Puella circuit. 6km/3.7mi; 1h35min. Easy, with a gradual ascent and short, fairly steep descent of 90m/295ft. While you *could* walk the 'official' Puella circuit up to Mont Agaisen (see purple highlighting on the map), our version is just a very easy ramble overlooking the eastern Bévéra basin, with fine views back

to Sospel. Follow the main walk to the school, then turn right (➤: *LA PUELLA*). Keep along the lane marked with yellow flashes, ignoring all turn-offs, until you come to ➤98, then turn down right for *SOSPEL PAR D2204*. This VTT route is very eroded, but quickly takes you to the D2204. Turn left and, at a junction, go right on the D93 in the **Nièya Valley** towards *VENTIMIGLIA*, passing **Le Golf**, the intriguing building which has been in sight throughout the walk. After 600m/yds, at ➤102, turn right on the GR510. A shady path and then a cart track take you via the lovely farm of **St-Gervais** back to the D2204 and the centre of Sospel.

Two things always delight us at Sospel — the wonderful freshness in the air and the Italianate atmosphere of the town, especially around the Place de la Cathédrale and along the banks of the rushing Bévéra River, where the richly-painted buildings are decorated with trompe l'oeil façades. Mont Agaisen affords you a fine view over the whole setting.

Start out in the centre of **Sospel** by crossing the *road* bridge over the **Bévéra River**. You look over to the right, to the 11th-century footbridge with its rebuilt toll tower (now the tourist office), flag a-flutter. Turn right on the far side, and follow this road for 200m/yds, then take steps up left to the Art Deco SCHOOL (➤72), from where you follow the GR52 (➤: *COL D'AGAISEN*).
When you come to ➤73, *ignore* the path on the right signposted to Agaisen; keep to the road. Turn

off the road at ➤74 (**15min**): follow the GR to the left up a gravel track, heading for *BAISSE DE FIGUEIRA*. Ignore two drives into houses almost immediately; keep left on the wide cart track. At the three-way fork that follows, take the middle route. There are lovely views left over olive groves and hillside terracing. At a Y-fork 10 minutes later, keep right. Soon the path moves into welcome shade and gently climbs a dry stream bed via a series of zigzags. As you rise, there's a specacular view south across the Sospel basin. Eventually a very short steep final burst brings you up to a three-way junction (**1h**). Take the road straight ahead (GR waymarks). Some 250m/yds further up, at ➤75, turn sharp right uphill for *BAISSE DE*

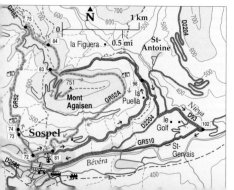

Fountain on the east side of the footbridge in Sospel (far left). The paths are mostly good underfoot, and in autumn Venetian sumac lights up the woodlands.

FIGUEIRA. A second ▐75 follows almost immediately: turn right for COL DE L'AGAISEN, where the GR52 to Baisse de Figueira curls up sharply to the left. From here the path undulates (keep straight ahead over a crossing path nine minutes along), finally descending to ▐84. Turn right here towards COL DE L'AGAISEN, immediately coming to a Y-fork. Keep to the wider path to the right. This beautiful section of path contours below pines and oaks.

On reaching a maze of paths and tracks at the **Col de l'Agaisen** (▐83; **1h30min**), you'll find a steep path straight ahead. *Ignore it* (it's the upper end of the path first passed at ▐73 and is used by VTTs). Take the wide track heading left, to the BLOCKHOUSE at the summit of **Mont Agaisen** (751m/2465ft; **1h50min**). Alpine hunters and riflemen were stationed here for many years from the late 1800s until 1939, to protect the border. There's a fine view of the Sospel basin ... and you *might* see some colourful hang-gliders.

From here return to ▐83 and now turn right on the path just below the track. Coming to a second ▐83 at a Y-fork, go half-right for SOSPEL VIA GR52A. This path

contours along the north side of the summit, then heads southeast through a sweetly-scented pine forest. The soft pine needles underfoot make this section very pleasant (photograph top right). You have a beautiful view down over the Short walk route in the Nièya Valley and out to the Bévéra Valley running through comfortable mountain folds towards Olivetta in Italy.

The narrow but good path is also used by VTTs and so is skiddy in places. Beyond a barn punctuated with cypress trees, follow the path straight over a road. When you meet the road again, follow it to the right and, after about 350m/yds, go sharp left down concrete steps. The ongoing path passes a little chapel with stained-glass windows.

The final descent is along the lovely stone-laid mule track shown above. A concrete ramp drops you down to ▐81 (**2h50min**); behind and to the left is the lane followed in the 'Puella' circuit (Short walk). From here you have a beautiful view to the church with its trompe l'oeil façade, together with two smaller churches. Back at the SCHOOL, turn left down the concrete steps, to the centre of **Sospel** (**3h**).

Walk 12: CIME DE L'ARPIHA

Distance: 9km/5.6mi; 2h40min
Grade: easy-moderate, with ascents/descents of about 280m/920ft; good tracks and paths. The scramble to the Arpiha summit demands some agility. Yellow PR waymarking. *IGN map 3741 ET*
Equipment: see page 61; refreshments available at Turini
How to get there: 🚗 (Car tour 2) or 🚐 340 (*only Sundays*) to the Col de Turini

Turini! One of the first places we make for when we arrive at Nice. Surrounded by magnificent forests of firs and spruce, this eyrie is as silent and refreshing as a Christmas morning snowfall … except when there's a motor rally on the famous hairpin road! Nearby are the gold-green mountains of the Authion (see box page 21), the backdrop for this walk.

Start out at the **Col de Turini:** walk north on the D68 (Authion road, signposted CAMP D'ARGENT).

After 700m/yds, at ⌐234 (**15min**), turn left. Follow this motorable track to the **Vacherie de Mantégas** (⌐235). From July to September you can sample and buy local cheeses here.
From the dairy farm continue towards *L'ARPIHA* on wide track (⌐: *ITINERAIRE*). When you come to a clearing at spot height 1648 (**30min**), signs point straight ahead to L'Arpiha. But we take the fork *half-left* here. This shady and mostly grassy path undulates along the south side of the Scoubayoun ridge. Breaks in the trees afford glimpses down left over Turini and the hairpin road. Be sure to keep right uphill at a fork 15 minutes along (as waymarked). At ⌐236 (**1h05min**), go straight ahead for *L'ARPIHA*. You come to a second ⌐236 at a grassy col. From here scramble up to the **Cime de l'Arpiha** (1634m/5360ft; **1h 25min**), to enjoy some magnificent views — west to the deeply-etched Planchette and Bollène valleys running towards the Vésubie, and east to the spread of the Authion massif.
Return to the *second* ⌐236 and turn left. This path rises 150m/495ft in deep shade to the highest point in the walk, the **Tête de Scoubayoun**, then drops 50m/165ft back to the clearing at spot height 1648. Turn left here, to retrace your steps back to the **Col de Turini** (**2h40min**).

The Authion from the Scoubayoun ridge

Walk 13: LAC DE TRECOLPAS AND REFUGE DE LA COUGOURDE

See map page 89
Distance: 10km/6.2mi; 4h20min
Grade: moderate-strenuous, with an ascent/descent of 520m/1700ft overall. The first half of the walk (up to Trécolpas Lake) is one long steady pull. Beyond the lake the walk levels out, before descending. Yellow PR, red and white GR waymarking. *IGN map 3741 OT*
Equipment: see page 61; binoculars. Make sure you have enough warm clothing. Refreshments available at Le Boréon
How to get there: 🚌 to the 'Parking supérieur du Boréon' (Car tour 2; route description on pages 19-20).
Short walk: Le Boréon — Pont de Peïrastrèche — Le Boréon. 3.5km/2.2mi; 1h40min. Fairly easy ascent/descent of 180m/600ft. Follow the main walk for 55min; return the same way.

Alternative walk *(expert grade):* Le Boréon — Lac de Trécolpas — Pas des Ladres — Madone de Fenestre. 9km/5.6mi; 5h15min. Strenuous climb of 800m/2625ft, followed by a descent of 550m/1800ft. Arrange for friends/a taxi to collect you at Madone de Fenestre and take you back to your car. Better, walk with friends who also have a car, and leave one car at Madone de Fenestre. Follow the main walk to the **Lac de Trécolpas** and from there continue on the GR52 to the **Pas des Ladres** *(the last part of this climb is a steep, difficult scramble on all fours).* At the pass pick up Walk 14 at the 2h20min-point, to descend to **Madone de Fenestre.**
Short walk/picnic suggestion: Chalet Vidron. 2.7km/1.7mi; 1h. Easy. Follow the main walk for 30 minutes and return the same way.

This is one of the most rewarding walks in the Mercantour, especially considering the little effort involved. There is ample shade on the lower slopes, and much of the walk follows a foaming stream. But the two highlights are the teal-blue Lac de Trécolpas and the magnificent rock bastion of La Cougourde. Throughout the walk be alert: you will find many pockets of alpine flora and almost certainly see chamois.

Start the walk at the **Parking supérieur du Boréon.** From ⌐420, head east on the wide earthen forest track that gently climbs through the **Vallon du Haut Boréon.** On coming to a fork (⌐421; **10min**), ignore the route up right to the Refuge de la Maïris; continue straight ahead. At another, Y-fork (⌐422; **15min**) follow the footpath to the right. Soon the summits where we are heading are visible, tinged with chartreuse lichen (see photograph page 90). When you hear the stream roaring below you, look ahead to the left through breaks in the trees, to see a lovely waterfall. Before long a wiggly watercourse

sidles up beside you on the left; follow it to the **Chalet Vidron** (**30min**), a stone hut beside a tiny lake. This is a delightful place for a picnic and, in late spring, you will find pockets of violets and gentians nearby.

From here follow PEÏRASTRÈCHE, LAC DE TRECOLPAS, PAS DES LADRES, climbing steeply in zig-zags. At a clearing where there is a chaos of boulders and a blanket of pine needles underfoot, it is easy to lose sight of the path. *It is worth spending some time* making sure you are on the correct route; there is a *good* path here, but there are *no* paint waymarks, only small cairns. (If you lose your way in the chaos,

head uphill and *slightly* right out of the clearing; keep away from the chaos of rock over to the far right. When you can, head left down towards the stream, to get to the bridge.) When you reach the top of the chaos you will be facing the scree-strewn slopes of Mont Pélago on the western side of the stream. If you have stayed on the cairned route, it will drop you down to the **Pont de Peïrastrèche** (**55min**).

Cross the bridge (another pleasant picnic spot) and quickly come to ⌐423. Follow *LACS BESSONS, REFUGE DE LA COUGOURDE, PAS DES LADRES*. Now you have joined the GR52 and soon begin climb-ing in earnest; watch for the red and white flashes as the path keeps hard by the banks of the stream. Ten minutes from the Pont de Peïrastrèche cross a makeshift LOG BRIDGE over a tributary, and a couple of minutes later wade across another. Cross another LOG BRIDGE (**1h10min**); with every step you draw nearer to the magnificent *cirque* before you. Five minutes later another BRIDGE is crossed, and another five minutes brings you to ⌐424 (**1h20min**): bear right for *LAC DE TRECOLPAS, PAS DES LADRES*, where a path goes left to the Lacs Bessons.

In another five minutes you approach a bridge on the right and ⌐425 (**1h25min**). The 'Route du Cougourde' (direct to the refuge which we will visit later) is off to

left; we go up *right* on the GR52 for PAS DES LADRES and LAC DE TRECOLPAS. Don't be alarmed if you seem to be heading back the way you came; soon the path heads due east and rises steeply. It's quite a huff-and-puff up to ☞427 (**2h10min**), so you will be relieved to know that your goal is just over the saddle ahead. Ten minutes later you reach the highest point of the walk (2187m/7175ft; **2h20min**). The exquisite **Lac de Trécolpas** is just below you here — and you may be surprised to find it frozen over, even in June! If you are climbing to the Pas des Ladres (Alternative walk), the GR52 continues from the north side of the lake.

From the lake return to ☞427 and go right for REFUGE DE LA COU-GOURDE. This level path first crosses a gigantic 'scree' of enor-mous boulders, but later the way is carpeted with soft pine needles. Soon a beacon shines out on the other side of the valley — the canary-yellow mountain hut. A gurgling stream is crossed on a makeshift bridge, and another stream is forded on stepping stones, before you finally reach the **Refuge de la Cougourde (2h 50min**). Idyllically perched beside the rushing stream, the refuge boasts a restaurant (in summer) and even a terrace!

Here ☞426 points back to the way you've come, but (at time of writing) *not* to the way down. Walk to the south-facing terrace of the refuge (shown in the photo-graph opposite) and you will see your ongoing path. It crosses the stream and then skirts to the right of it. The good path descends steeply, sometimes on stone steps, and skips over many streams via stepping stones or logs.

Beyond a grassy basin you come back to ☞425 (**3h20min**). Follow LE BOREON now, to return along your outgoing route. (Just ahead on the left is a water trough where you may see chamois; *go quietly*.) After recrossing the Pont de Peïrastrèche be sure to take the lower path on the right. Descend through the cairned chaos; the route is more easily seen in this direction. Return past the Chalet Vidron to ☞420 at the **Parking supérieur du Boréon (4h20min**).

The Lac de Trécolpas, seen from the Pas des Ladres (Walk 14 and Alternative walk 13). The Caïre des Gaisses and La Cougourde rise behind the lake, not far from the Italian border. In fact the Mercantour reserve was originally created by the King of Italy as hunting grounds and to protect chamois. Even when the County of Nice (to which the Mercantour was attached) was returned to France in 1860, the Italian king was allowed to keep his 'réserve de chasse'. Only with the Treaty of Paris in 1947 did the border revert to the Alpine watershed (see also Walk 14).

Walk 14: COL DE FENESTRE AND PAS DES LADRES

See photographs pages 8-9, 86-87, 90 (bottom)
Distance: 8km/5mi; 3h40min
Grade: fairly strenuous, with an ascent/descent of 600m/2000ft. Stony terrain underfoot. Beyond the Col de Fenestre the footpath demands some agility. *No shade.* Red and white GR, yellow PR waymarking. *IGN map 3741 OT*
Equipment: see page 61; binoculars. Make sure you have enough warm clothing. Refreshments available at St-Martin-Vésubie (13km)
How to get there: 🚌 to the CAF

refuge at Madone de Fenestre (Car tour 2; the road is 200m north-west of St-Martin-Vésubie centre).

Short walk: Madone de Fenestre — Lac de Fenestre — Madone de Fenestre. 5.5km/3.4mi; 2h. Easy-moderate ascent/descent of 370m/1200ft on a good trail (stout shoes will suffice). Follow the main walk to the lake; return the same way.

Alternative walk *(expert grade):* Le Boréon — Lac de Trécolpas — Pas des Ladres — Madone de Fenestre. See Alternative walk 13, page 85.

This classic walk is steeped in history. It is thought that a Roman temple and travellers' shelter once existed near the spot where the chapel now stands at Madone de Fenestre. But the trail we follow to the Col de Fenestre predates even Roman times. For a thousand years, until the end of World War II, this route was often a battleground. Even in the 16th century, when both sides of the col belonged to the House of Savoy, the breach was closed in a vain effort to stop the plague spreading south from Piedmont to Nice. The detritus of World War II, barbed wire, rubble and bunkhouses, still menaces the Col de Fenestre, which today marks the border with Italy.

Start the walk at **Madone de Fenestre**: climb the steps at the left of the large CAF refuge, to find ▐357. Turn right for *PAS DES LADRES* along the wide, very stony trail (red and white flashes of the GR52). The stream roars away below on the right, beside the Vacherie de la Madone. A splendid *cirque* rises before you, dominated by the summit of Mount Gélas (photograph pages 8-9). At a Y-fork just beyond ▐368 (**25min**), bear right for *LAC DE FENESTRE* (the GR52, our return route, climbs left here). You quickly ford a stream. Fifteen minutes later a beautiful grassy slope makes a lovely rest stop, from where you look out southeast to the pointed Petit Caïre and the larger Caïre de la Madone. Then trudge on. Your

pack-horse plodding is rewarded when you reach the glistening **Lac de Fenestre** (**1h05min**), a good place to end the Short walk with a picnic.

Continue ahead towards 2000 years of history, climbing below the needle-sharp heights of the Cime Est de Fenestre. Some 10 minutes beyond the lake, ignore the path off to the left; keep right. Look up left to the western summit of Fenestre (Cime Ouest) with its crenellated silhouette. Pass below a *BUNKER* up on your left, and then a second *BUNKER* on your right. They were built by the Italians during World War II. At a crossing path (▐369; **1h 45min**), go right uphill to the **Col de Fenestre** (2471m/8105ft; **1h 50min**), where there is another

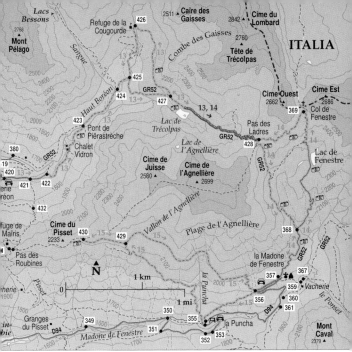

bunker, a cross and a boundary stone. From here a waymarked path continues into Italy. Looking down the wide valley below the Cime du Lombard on the left, it is easy to appreciate why this was a major gateway between France and Italy for thousands of years. Return to ⌐369 and go straight ahead for *REFUGE DE COUGOURDE, LAC DE TRECOLPAS, PAS DES LADRES*. This narrow path, which requires some agility, offers good views back over the Lac de Fenestre and, on clear days, towards the sparkling Mediterranean. On the final part of the ascent, just when the Lac de Fenestre is out of sight, you head towards the summit of Mount Agnellière, then look northwest to the deep gash of the Boréon Valley (Walk 13), with Mount Pélago beyond it. When the walk flattens out, it is easy to lose the path amongst the rocks — if you do, look slightly downhill to the west, and you will spot the wooden fingerpost at the pass.

Soon you're at the **Pas des Ladres** (**2h20min**), looking down over Trécolpas Lake from the vantage point shown on pages 86-87. ⌐428 indicates the path up from the lake (Alternative walk 13) and another path to the summit of Agnellière rising in the southwest. Turn left down a narrow path in front of a huge cairn (GR flashes; ⌐: *MADONE DE FENESTRE*). Very quickly, turn back sharp left downhill, where the Agnellière path goes straight ahead. As you descend, the Lac de Fenestre comes into view again, and the wide trail followed earlier stands out like a highway.

After dropping down to ford a stream on stepping stones, the path levels out and crosses a scree. As you approach the Petit Caïre again, notice the gulley you crossed on the way up, where moss hangs from the rocks like a wispy beard.

Back at ⌐368 (**3h15min**), retrace your outgoing trail to **Madone de Fenestre** (**3h40min**).

89

Walk 15: CIME DU PISSET

See map page 89
Distance: 9km/5.6mi; 3h40min
Grade: fairly strenuous, with an
ascent/descent of 580m/1900ft.
You must be sure-footed and agile.
Little shade. Yellow PR waymark-
ing, some green hexagons. *IGN
map 3741 OT*
Equipment: as Walk 14, page 88
How to get there: 🚌 to the La
Puncha picnic table on the
Madone de Fenestre road (Car
tour 2; see page 20).

*The contour path along the Plage de
l'Agnellière looks deceptively easy, but
you may find landslips in the many
tributary valleys. Below: lichen-clad
slopes above Madone de Fenestre*

This lovely walk offers a maximum of 'balcony' views for
minimum effort — when compared with other hikes in
the Mercantour! From the Cime du Pisset, the Boréon and
Madone de Fenestre valleys open out below you.

Start the walk below the **La
Puncha** picnic table, on the north
side of the road (⊓355). Following
CIME DU PISSET, ignore a trail on
the right to Madone de Fenestre
(the return route). The path climbs
due north up the **Vallon de la
Puncha**; the zigzags and good
shade on this stretch help you gain
300m/1000ft in height quite
quickly. The path then emerges on
bare mountain flanks and rises
northwest, now climbing less
steeply.
When you reach ⊓429, you're
almost at the highest point in the
climb (2200m/7220ft; **1h45min**).
From here it's just short detour
west up to the viewpoint on the
Cime du Pisset (⊓430; **2h**).

Return to ⊓429 and begin to contour southeast along the **Plage de
l'Agnellière** on a 'balcony' path
above the Vallon de Fenestre
(large green hexagonal waymarks).
You will come across screes at all
the stream bed crossings on this
traverse, *most* of them stabilised.
After the final stream bed, *there are
no further waymarks:* remember, as
you approach Madone de Fenestre,
that your goal is *not* the buildings
— the path zigzags down to the
road well *before* the deep stream
bed and scree separating you from
the CAF refuge.
When you meet the road (⊓356;
3h15min), turn right and follow
the lovely old pilgrims' trail back
down to **La Puncha** (**3h40min**).

Walk 16: CASCADE DE L'ESTRECH

Above: the bounding stream in the upper Gordolasque Valley; below: Pont du Countet, where the walk begins

Distance: 5.5km/3.4mi; 2h35min
Grade: moderate climb of 340m/1115ft on stony paths; agility required. *No shade.* Yellow PR waymarking. *IGN map 3741 OT*
Equipment: as Walk 14, page 88. Refreshments available at St-Grat (3km) and Belvédère (13km)
How to get there: 🚐 to car park at the end of the road in the Gordolasque Valley (Car tour 2).

Alternative walk: Refuge de Nice. 11km/6.8mi; 4h. Grade as main walk, with a climb/descent of 540m/1770ft. At the 1h15min-point in the main walk, continue ahead via ⌐415 and ⌐416 to the **Lac de la Fous** and CAF refuge (refreshments available in summer). Return the same way and pick up the main walk again.
Note: The most famous walk in the Mercantour — to the **Vallée des Merveilles**, where there are more than 30,000 Bronze Age petroglyphs — can be done in a day starting here at the Pont du Countet and climbing via the Pas de l'Arpette to the GR52. This is a day-long, tough walk, and certain areas are only accessible to walkers with an approved guide. To make the most of this hike (some of the engravings are hard to find), you could walk with a guided group: enquire at the tourist office in St-Martin or Belvédère. If you walk on your own, obtain the Park pamphlet showing the restricted areas. *IGN map 3741 OT*

91

If you're not doing *the* walk from the Gordolasque (to the Vallée des Merveilles), this short alternative is a delight. It takes you above a gorgeous waterfall, in a setting where you may be tempted to linger all day.

Start out at the CAR PARK: walk through the open barrier, to the walkers' signboards. Don't cross the **Pont du Countet**; take the stony track to the left (⌐: ECOLE D'ESCALADE). Now edge along the stream, in an idyllic setting of cascades and grassy banks. Perhaps the *cirque* ahead will be flecked with snow. Not far beyond the chaos of high boulders used by the climbing school, begin to rise on a narrow path. Soon the waterfall is seen up ahead. To its right, a rock cliff (Mur des Italiens) seems to close off the valley.

At ⌐413 (**25min**) a path goes right, across the river, to Lac Autier and the Mur des Italiens. You will return across this bridge at the end of the walk, but for now swing up left into the first of the hairpin bends on the lower slopes of **Mont Neiglier**. Cairns mark the route where it passes over bedrock. As you reach the final hairpin bend to the left (**1h**), first walk over to the right for a good

view of the bounding **Cascade de l'Estreche**. When the path levels out (**1h10min**), you will see another path on the far side of the river, below the Mur des Italiens. Soon you can cross the steam on STEPPING STONES (**1h15min**) to join it. *(But for the Alternative walk, keep straight ahead.)*

Now heading back south below the 'Italians' Wall', you walk through the walls of a RUINED FORTIFICATION and later pass a massive CAIRN, overlooking a beautiful teal-blue RIVER POOL (**1h45min**).

At ⌐414 (**1h55min**), ignore the earthen path climbing ahead to Lac Autier; go right downhill on the wider stony path, towards the river. On reaching the old electricity workers' road (⌐413; just over **2h**), head down steps, cross the **Gordolasque Stream** on the bridge you spotted earlier, and retrace your outgoing route back to the **Pont du Countet** and CAR PARK (**2h35min**).

The hamlet of St-Grat, backed by the cirque *at the head of the valley*

Walk 17: CIRCUIT FROM GOURDON

Distance: 9km/5.6mi; 3h
Grade: fairly easy, with a steep, very stony descent of 200m/650ft at the start and a gradual ascent of under 300m/1000ft near the end. Red and white GR, yellow PR and some magenta waymarking. *IGN map 3643 ET*
Equipment: see page 61; binoculars; a *torch is essential.* Refreshments available at Gourdon
How to get there: 🚌 (Car tour 3) or 🚐 to Gourdon
Alternative walk: Gourdon — Le Bar-sur-Loup. 4km/2.5mi; 2h. Fairly easy, but initially steep and stony, descent of 450m/1475ft; no torch needed. Yellow waymarks. At the 30min-point in the main walk cross over the **Aqueduc du Foulon** and keep descending until you come to the **Aqueduc du Loup**, where you turn right. After 25 minutes along this level path turn left downhill (⌐: LE BAR). A stone-laid trail takes you to the **Chapelle St-Claude**. Walk along-

side the CEMETERY, then follow the Chemin de la Bessurane and Rue du Ribas to the centre. Return to Gourdon by taxi (11km) or climb back the same way (2h30min). If scheduling permits, you can also take a 🚐 from here to Grasse and then a 🚐 back to Gourdon.

The first part of this walk, a descent on the aptly-named 'Paradise Trail', is an extravaganza of bird's-eye views down over the lush Loup Valley and the coast. We then follow a piped watercourse through aromatic pines, in the company of butterflies and dark red squirrels. At the end of the walk, there is a gradual climb under the pleasant shade of oaks.

Start out at the CAR PARK/BUS STOP below **Gourdon**; walk up towards the village, but fork left on a path to the WC (before the centre). Past the WC, at the end of this path, steps take you down into the **Gourdon Valley** on an old mule trail, the **Chemin du Paradis**. In five minutes, you come to a wide rocky ledge, a superb picnic spot overlooking the coast. The Montagne de Courmettes rises on the far side of the Loup Gorge (where you may spot paragliders). Notice the piers of the old viaduct, destroyed in World War II, and the large water pipe below — your ongoing route.

When you meet the fat old rusty pipe (**Aqueduc du Foulon; 30min**), turn right alongside it (⌐: GRASSE). *(The Alternative walk continues straight ahead downhill here.)* You will follow this pipe, in the company of the red and white flashes of the GR51, for just under an hour (keep your torch handy for the tunnels). Whenever there is a break in the trees, you enjoy a fine outlook over the coast (the wedge-shaped apartments at Baie des Anges can serve as a landmark: they are just west of Cagnes and east of Antibes).

A particularly fine outlook comes up just as the aqueduct rounds a

93

bend: you have a perfect view down over Le Bar and along the whole sweep of coast from the hills behind Eze to the Maures. Now, as you head west, the path rounds an steep escarpment, protected by railings.

On coming to a 'crossroads' (**1h 25min**), turn right up a steep concreted lane. On your left, olive groves grace a deep basin. Four minutes later, ignore the left fork back to the canal; follow the GR uphill to the right, on the concrete lane. But six minutes later, when the GR heads off to the left, keep *straight ahead* on a tarmac lane (◼: BOIS DE GOURDON). After another five minutes turn left off this lane: go up STEPS (◼: BOIS DE GOURDON; **1h40min**). Now *carefully* follow *magenta* waymarks along a narrow path through oaks and spring-flowering broom. When you come to a crossing cart track (**1h50min**), follow it to the left (MAGENTA ARROW). After several paces, another track curves in front of you at a T-junction: turn left here, on a rough concrete lane. You pass a huge PIT in half a minute and then cross the D3 (**1h 53min**). On the far side of the road, continue behind a barrier on a gravel track to the left of a CIS-TERN. Five minutes later, be sure to turn off this fire-break track, going left on a stony trail (posts with magenta waymarks at the outset). As you climb this lovely

94

woodland trail, ignore two paths off left (after one minute and four minutes later). Soon look right through the trees: you are level with Gourdon on the far side of the valley. This woodland was once the hunting grounds of the Counts of Gourdon … and the scene of violent clashes between the inhabitants of Gourdon and Le Bar, both of whom claimed the right to collect its wood.

On coming to a strong crossing stony trail (**2h15min**), *go straight over*, even though there are *no way-marks* ahead. Five minutes later cross straight over the fire-break onto a path (there is a huge screened-off APIARY on the left). Five minutes past the apiary, an old stone-laid trail comes in from the left; continue to the right, straight towards the Loup Gorge. In a minute you join a good gravel track: turn right. Now the walk, again in full sun, descends gradually across a plateau, with more spectacular views — to Gourdon, the Loup cleft and the coast. You pass a CROSS on the left near a QUARRY and then cross a BRIDGE. Tarmac comes underfoot and you meet the D12: head right, back to the CAR PARK (**3h**).

Now visit well-restored **Gourdon**, not missing the *table d'orientation* behind the church. The 13/14th-century castle, built on the foundations of a Saracen fortress, houses a history museum and a gallery of naïve art. If you are unable to resist all the craft shops, at least you won't have to lug all your souvenirs round the Loup Valley!

Walk 18: CASTELLARAS

Distance: 3km/2mi; 1h30min
Grade: fairly easy climb and descent of 245m/800ft, but the paths are quite stony. Yellow PR waymarking. *IGN map 3542 ET*
Equipment: see page 61; refreshments available at Thorenc (2km)
How to get there: 🚗 to a small parking area on the D2 (0.6km west of the junction with the D5, at ⌐145; Car tours 3, 4)

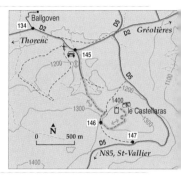

E ast of Thorenc, between the Lane and Loup valleys, an impressive plinth of rock rises above the D2, crowned by the remains of a 12th-century castle. The site dominates one of the finest panoramas in the Grasse Pre-Alps, and it is probable that a Ligurian *oppidum* existed here as early as 600BC.

Start out at ⌐145; follow the track running south, rising through box and stunted pines gnarled into whimsical 'bonsai' shapes. Soon a huge doorway appears in the crest above. At a fork (**12min**), go right — you'll spot a yellow waymark a couple of minutes later. Ignore a stony path down left to the D5 (**20min**); turn sharp right. Five minutes later, at a grassy SADDLE strewn with wild flowers, you come upon ⌐146, where another path leads south to the D5. Climb up left to the **Castellaras** (**50min**), passing through its 2ft-thick drystone walls. Explore the château, towers, and vaulted chapel. Then take in the vast panorama. Bauroux (Walk 22) rises in the west, the Col de

Bleine with its relay in the north and Cheiron in the northeast. In the south the Audibergue dominates the Loup Valley, which can be traced southeast to its gorge and the Col de Vence.
Then retrace your steps to ⌐145 (**1h30min**).

The Castellaras

Walk 19: SOURCE DE LA SIAGNOLE

See also photo page 133 (top)
Distance: 10.5km/6.5mi; 2h25min
Grade: easy ascent/descent of
under 100m/330ft overall, but
requiring some agility on narrow
paths. Red and white GR waymarking. *IGN map 3543 ET*
Equipment: see page 61 (trainers
will suffice); refreshments available
at Mons (7km)
How to get there: 🚌 to the
bridge over the Siagnole at Les
Moulins (D56, 6.8km south of the
parking area in Mons; Car tour 4)
Short walks
1 **Chapelle St-Peire.** 4.5km/
2.8mi; 1h20min. Easy. Follow the
main walk for 40min and return
the same way.
2 **Source de la Siagnole.** 2km/
1.2mi; 50min. Easy. Walk to the

sign LA SIAGNOLE on the south side
of the bridge and turn right just
beyond it, climbing a steep, sometimes mucky path. At a fork two-
three minutes uphill, go left. In a
minute or two you meet a major
footpath (by some FLUORESCENT
RED WAYMARKS); turn right. This
sometimes narrow path (watch
your footing) covers the old
ROMAN AQUEDUCT; at one point
you will have to squat down under
a rock overhang. Go through a
first BARRIER (barring motorbikes)
and walk ahead past a second
barrier, to the left of a SHELTER;
then keep ahead to the fenced-in
Source de la Siagnole (25min). If
you wish to picnic, refer to the
main walk notes at the 1h50min-
point. Return the same way.

This beautiful walk above the gorges of the Siagnole,
mostly in the shade of oaks, is perfect for a hot day. Before
setting off, visit the *table d'orientation* in Mons, to identify all
the landmarks in the area.

Start out at **Les Moulins.** Cross
the bridge over the **Siagnole** and
walk south along the D56 for
500m/yds, then turn left off the
road on a footpath (GR waymarks;
some agility is required here).
Soon you're walking through the
rock passage shown on page 133
(**Roche Taillée; 12min**), hewn
out by the Romans to accommodate a watercourse. Now you
follow the GR49 along a earthen
path atop the aqueduct, in the
shade of oaks.
When the GR heads uphill to the
right (under **20min**), *keep ahead*
(the GR path is the *return* route).
Four minutes later ignore another
path off to the right. Breaks in the
foliage permit fine views over to
Mons and down the gorge towards
St-Cézaire, setting for Walk 21.
Eventually (**35min**) the path
swings away from the Siagnole
and you join a grassy track. Keep
straight ahead. Two minutes later,

on coming to a T-junction with an
earthen track, turn left. Almost
immediately, you walk through an
opening in a stone wall, past a
WINDMILL on your right, and to
the tiny **Chapelle St-Peire**, shown
opposite (**40min**). Both are on
private land, near a cottage, so it's
best not to linger.
Return to the track and go left
(west). Ignore tracks to the left
and then the right; keep to this
main track, following the electricity wires. When you reach a
Y-fork (**55min**), bear right to the
D37, and turn right. Walk ahead
to a sign indicating a crossroads
and, 75m/yds beyond the sign,
turn right on a footpath, crushing
wild herbs underfoot as you go.
This short-cut path takes you to
the D56, where you turn right for
20 paces and then pick up the GR
again, on your right. Descending
through *garrigues,* the pretty path
affords fine views over to the bald

Chapelle St-Peire (top) and the Siagnole near the source

summits of the Audibergue. When the GR drops you back down to the AQUEDUCT at the point first passed 20min into the walk (**1h10min**), turn *sharp left*. (Straight ahead leads back to the St-Piere chapel.) Retrace your outgoing route back through the **Roche Taillée** to the D56 (**1h 20min**). Cross the road and continue along the GR49. You are still atop the aqueduct, on a lovely shady path. Ignore all paths and trails to the left and right. Soon the Siagnole makes its presence felt, burbling along on your right, in the shadow of the Valbouissole cliffs. Pass through a first BARRIER (**1h45min**) and shortly, a second BARRIER, by a concrete HUT. The path ends in front of the fenced-off **Source de la Siagnole** (**1h50min**). To reach the source (and a lovely picnic place), return to the BARRIER WITH THE HUT and turn left downhill on a steep and slippery trail just beyond it. This takes you to a FORD which is easily crossed (*unless the stream is running high*).* Turn left on the cart track on the far side,

*There is also a footbridge just downstream from this point, but it is gated and often *locked*; if you returned from the picnic area to find

to a stand of very tall oaks and a circle of boulder 'seats'. Nearby is the SOURCE itself, behind a small metal gate bearing the date 1918. From here retrace your steps past the BARRIER WITH THE HUT to the next BARRIER, then turn left at the Y-fork of paths (still on the GR; you descended the path to the right here). You are now on the lower aqueduct and the path is just as attractive, cool with moss and ivy and the sound of the river tinkling beside you on the left. Five minutes along, when the aqueduct rounds a steep escarpment, railings protect the drop to the left, but you have to squat down under an overhang of rock, chiselled out by the Romans. *Watch your footing.*

Six minutes past the railings, turn left down a steep, mucky path, following FLUORESCENT RED WAYMARKS (the GR keeps straight ahead here). Below, through the trees, you can see Les Moulins. Ignore the path down left three minutes into the descent (it goes to the mill); keep straight ahead. A minute later you meet the D56: turn left, back to the BRIDGE at **Les Moulins** (**2h25min**).

the bridge locked, you would have to follow the cart track via Les Gombauds back to the D56 (see map.)

Walk 20: GORGES DU BLAVET

Distance: 7.5km/4.7mi; 2h
Grade: easy descent/ascent of 170m/560ft. White PR, red and white GR waymarking. *IGN map 3544 ET*
Equipment: see page 61; refreshments available at Bagnols
How to get there: Approaching Bagnols on the D47 (Car tour 4), watch out for the Chapelle Notre-Dame (with 🏠) on your right, just before the wine co-op. Turn right here. After 100m turn right on the Chemin

Colle Rousse from the Bayonne circuit

de Bayonne. Park at the Castel de Bayonne, 1.7km beyond a TV mast.

This walk is memorable for its fine views of red-rock cliffs, the sweetly-scented *maquis*, and the pretty rock pools in the Gorges du Blavet. On fine days you'll also have a splendid outlook to the Rocher de Roquebrune rising in the south.

Start out at the **Castel de Bayonne**: walk back downhill (the way you came). A few metres/yards beyond the end of the fencing encircling the property, turn *sharp* left downhill on a clear but narrow footpath (white dot waymarks). The gently-descending path runs through typical *maquis*, before the landscape opens out to give fine views west to the Colle Rousse (20min). Later the path widens out amidst pines and heather; the Bayonne summit rises on the left.

When you come to a stony crossing trail (33min), follow it to the right (the way to the left is your return route). Three minutes later you reach WATER TANK No 1, on the right. Here take the stony trail to the left (🏠: *GORGES DU BLAVET*). Pass a field on the right, beyond

which the Colle Rousse rises in the background. On coming to a Y-fork, go left (the way to the right *may* be marked with an 'X'). Under 10 minutes from the tank you meet a wide crossing path waymarked in the red and white flashes of the GR51 (45min). Follow it to the left downhill, descending to the RIVER POOLS in the **Gorges du Blavet** (50min). From here the GR crosses the river, but retrace your steps to WATER TANK NO 1 (1h10min), and turn right on the stony trail. Rising gently, in four minutes you pass the path you descended earlier in the walk. Ignore a path off left to the Bayonne summit (1h25min), then take a break at the beautiful outcrop of red rock on the right — looking out to the gorges and the massive Rocher de Roquebrune on the far side of the Argens Valley.

Five minutes past this viewpoint keep left at a fork (GR waymarks). Ten minutes later, go left again (still on the GR). Go straight over the next crossroads (eight minutes later), to pass WATER TANK NO 10 on the right (1h50min). Just another 10 minutes uphill, past fields full of autumn-flowering heather, you're back at the **Castel de Bayonne** (2h).

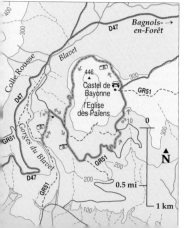

Walk 21: GORGES DE LA SIAGNE

Distance: 9.5km/6mi; 3h
Grade: moderate-strenuous, with descents/ascents of 440m/1445ft overall. Some of the stony paths require agility. Yellow PR, red and white GR waymarking. *IGN map 3543 ET*
Equipment: see page 61; swimming things. Refreshments available at St-Cézaire-sur-Siagne
How to get there: 🚌 or 🚗 to St-Cézaire-sur-Siagne (Car tour 4); park at the 'Chapelle Romane' (N-D de Sardaigne), south of the D13, on the southeast side of the village.

Alternative walk: Pont des Tuves and Pont des Moulins. 8km/ 5mi; 2h45min. Moderate, with a descent and re-ascent of 310m/ 1015ft requiring agility. Follow the main walk to ┌7 and turn right on the short-cut path. Zigzag down to ┌8, where you join the GR510. Turn right to ┌9 and descend (crossing the **Canal de la Siagne**) to the **Pont des Tuves**. Cross the bridge and turn right on a yellow-waymarked path. This undulates above the river, passing the ruins of the **Tour de Siagne** and then a paper mill. Cross the **Pont des Moulins** and, on the far side, rise up to the canal again. Now you have a choice: *either* continue ahead (yellow waymarks) on the old road between St-Cézaire and Callian *or* turn right along the canal and follow it

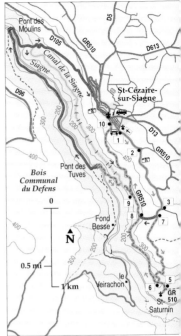

back to the yellow-waymarked descent path to the Pont des Tuves, climb up to the GR (7min) and turn left back to St-Cézaire. *The second option is always our choice,* but you must reckon on an *additional* 3km/2mi; 45min.
Note: This is just one of *many* alternatives around St-Cézaire. The tourist office has a useful leaflet of waymarked routes showing signpost numbers.

Almost all walks from St-Cézaire eventually cross the Canal de la Siagne ... and that's a big problem for us! We're so distracted and enchanted by this beautiful watercourse that we abandon all plans for a 'proper' walk and end up just following the canal. If you love the canals of Provence as much as we do, then be sure to pack a torch, so you can follow this one for as long as you like. And do it *soon* — they've told us in the village that the canal is to be covered with concrete!

The walk begins at the lovely Romanesque **Chapelle N-D de Sardaigne** in **St-Cézaire**. Take the lane on the south side of the

building (┌1), the **Chemin des Puits de Chautard**. After 500m/yds (at ┌2), turn right on another lane, the **Chemin du**

99

Pont des Tuves over the Siagne

Canal de la Siagne

Courbon. Descending between stone walls, you overlook the **Siagne Valley**, where a wonderful view opens up northwest along the gorge. At a fork 700m/yds along, keep right downhil, past beautiful houses set in terraced olive groves. At ⊩3 (**20min**), keep right on the forestry track. Almost immediately, at another fork (⊩7), keep left. *(But for the Alternative walk, take the path to the right, which zigzags straight down to the canal.)* You soon leave the track, to take a path on the right, continuing more or less in the same direction. Ignoring a wide path to the left signposted to Tuves, zigzag fairly steeply downhill, crossing the **Canal de la Siagne**, to ⊩6, where you join the GR510. Follow the GR to the left for 200m/yds; then,

at ⊩5, descend to the **Chapelle Saint-Saturnin** (**1h**). Return to ⊩6 and now follow the GR up the valley, recrossing the canal. At ⊩8 the short-cut path from ⊩7 comes in from the right. At ⊩9, keep left downhill, leaving the GR and following yellow waymarks. You cross the canal yet again and descend to the beautiful **Pont des Tuves** (**1h45min**). After taking a break in this lovely setting, return to ⊩9 and turn left for ST-CEZAIRE. This old donkey trail doesn't offer much shade, and although it's beautifully graded, it still takes almost an hour to rise up to the centre of **St-Cézaire** (**3h**). Wander around the lovely village, take in the view from the *table d'orientation* and then return to the **Chapelle N-D de Sardaigne**.

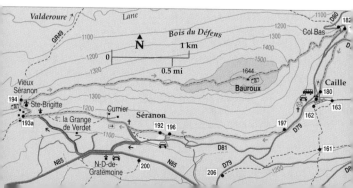

Walk 22: SERANON AND THE BAUROUX RIDGE

See map opposite; see also cover photograph

Distance: 13km/8mi; 4h45min

Grade: quite strenuous, with ascents/descents of 650m/2130ft overall. The descent path requires agility and *confidence;* less experienced walkers should retrace their steps from the summit. Red and white GR, yellow PR way-marking. *IGN map 3542 ET*

Equipment: see page 61; walking stick(s). Refreshments available at Séranon and Caille

How to get there: 🚌 to Séranon (Car tour 4; park in the square) or 🚐 to Caille; alight at the post office and start the walk at the 4h15min-point.

Short walks: We especially recommend three routes, each easy and taking under 2h. 1) follow the main walk to **Vieux Séranon** and back; 2) climb from **N-D-de-Gratemoine** to the **Chapelle Ste-Brigitte** or to **Vieux Séranon** and return via the Séranon cemeteries

The Route Napoléon from Vieux Séranon

(park at N-D-de-Gratemoine on the N85 and see the purple line on the map); 3) take the beautiful cart track from **Caille** to **Séranon** and back (🚌 or 🚐 to Caille; then pick up the main walk at the 4h15min-point).

Of all the landscapes in the south of France, one of the most magical for us is the chapel of Notre-Dame-de-Gratemoine on the Route Napoléon below Séranon (cover photograph). How many times we've picnicked there, looking up at the magnificent crest of Bauroux! This long walk leads you gently to the tremendous summit viewpoint and then drops you (literally) back down to Caille's grassy valley.

The walk begins in the village square in **Séranon**: follow GR waymarks to the north side of the village and ➤192 (*RUINES DU VIEUX SERANON*). Ignoring the lane, take the grassy path uphill here, just to the right of some houses. Pass some ruins on the left, then join a cart track and continue in the same direction. When you come to the CEMETERY, turn right, keeping the cemetery to your left. Join a road and follow it uphill to the right, passing above the old cemetery below on the left. When the lane curls right up to the hamlet of **Curnier**, keep left on a path (➤:

CHAPELLE STE-BRIGITTE). One minute later, at a Y-fork, you can either take the grassy cart track on the right or the GR path at the left. They rejoin just before the **Chapelle Ste-Brigitte** (**45min**), a fine place for a break.

Beyond the chapel keep ahead for BAUROUX (➤193a). Three minutes from the signpost you come to the first ruins of **Vieux Séranon**. The path passes to the left of the huge buttressed church and continues steeply uphill to the TOP OF THE LONG BAUROUX RIDGE (**1h**). Follow the path straight ahead towards VALDEROURE, but leave it

101

At the Bauroux summit

(*and* the GR) a minute later at ⊩194: turn right for BAUROUX, now following yellow PR way-marks. This path, just below the north side of the crest, rises slowly for well over 3km through the thickly-wooded **Bois du Défens**, affording only brief glimpses down into the Lane Valley. It's a long way to go without views, but the mossy path, with soft pine needles underfoot is cool and pleasant. *Finally* you spot some poles ahead, bright with 'signal flags' — these mark the SUMMIT OF **Bauroux** (1644m/5392ft; **2h45min**). Fling yourself down in the golden grass and absorb the breath-taking views down over the green, green plains below you — the valleys of the Lane and the Loup.

Now the real fun begins. The path down the northeast side of the mountain is marked with yellow flashes (and, later, plastic tags on rocks). Wait till you see the postage-stamp village of Caille straight below you from the edge of the ridge! Soon the path just drops through a rock chaos, where you'll spend a lot of time on all

fours (and probably searching in vain for waymarks). Just keep down, down, and you will come back to the main path, which eventually descends gently below pines. When you come to two WATER TANKS, circle half-way round them, then turn sharp right down a cart track. Meeting the D80 at **Col Bas** (**4h**), turn left to ⊩181 and there go right on a track towards CAILLE. Just before a property, curl left, down towards the D79. Turn right on this road and, after 150m/yds, turn left on a concrete drive. At a Y-fork, keep left on a cart track which passes to the left of a house. *Before* reaching the house, go left down a path. It widens to a lane and you pass to the left of the CEMETERY walls and rise to ⊩180 in **Caille**. Take steps on the right up to a road and turn left. Then turn right uphill in front of the MAIRIE, and pass to the left of the CHURCH and to the right of ⊩162. Keep ahead to a junction, join the D79 and follow it straight ahead, past the POST OFFICE on the right (**4h15min**). (This is where you start the walk if you come by bus.) Pass an IRON CROSS on your right and, 300m/yds further on (at ⊩197), take a cart track on the right. All the forks along this track are well waymarked. Looking up to the right, you should be able to spot the poles at the Bauroux summit. The trail descends gently amid the lush valley scenery, to **Séranon** (**4h45min**).

The Lane and Loup valleys, from the Bauroux summit

Walk 23: LAC D'ALLOS

See also photographs page 32
Distance: 8km/5mi; 2h35min
Grade: easy ascent/descent of
200m/650ft. Yellow/green PR
waymarking. *IGN map 3540 ET*
Equipment: see page 61; swimming things; warm clothing in
cold weather. Refreshments
available in Allos or at the Lac
d'Allos (in high season)
How to get there: 🚗 to the Lac
d'Allos car park (Car tour 5)
Short walk: Lac d'Allos. 5.5km/
3.4mi; 1h50min. Grade as main
walk. Follow the main walk, but
omit the circuit of the lake.
*Note: Dogs are not allowed on this
walk.*

Beautifully laid out as a nature trail, this walk in the most
westerly valley of the Mercantour National Park is a
fascinating introduction to Alpine geology. But *don't* just
follow everyone else straight to the lake; first come with us to
a high plateau of breathtaking beauty — where, in summer,
you are guaranteed to see bushy-tailed marmots galore.

Start out at the PARKING AREA
below the lake: follow the stony
path (**⬤**: LAC D'ALLOS) up past a
forestry house. The **Chadoulin
Stream** rushes by on the right.
Beyond a WILLOW GROVE, planted
to prevent erosion of the stream
banks, you cross a tributary, the
Méouille, and join a track.
Soon an information panel calls
your attention to some lichen-
encrusted rocks (**15min**). A
minute later, turn sharp left up a
path (**⬤**: MONT PELAT). (The track,
your return route, continues ahead
to the lake.) This shady path
climbs quickly above the Ravin de
Méouille down to the left, and you
come upon a gorgeous amphitheatre — a meadow surrounded
by high mountains, guaranteed to
impart that fantastic 'top-of-the-
world' feeling. On a hot day there
is ample shade for picnicking here;
on a cool day it's a sun trap. If you
look right, you can see the Tours
du Lac on the far side of the Lac

d'Allos. Walk across the meadow,
straight towards the pyramids of
the Trou de l'Aigle and Mont Pélat
(photograph page 32).
On reaching a signpost (spot
height 2259m; **40min**), turn
sharp right for LAC D'ALLOS,
ignoring a path left to Mount
Pélat and another half right to the
Col de la Cayolle. When the grassy
path approaches a ROCK CHAOS
WITH A SHEEPFOLD, follow the
yellow and green waymarks
carefully: you must keep this
moraine (boulders plucked up and
deposited by the glacier) *to your
left*. Soon you enjoy a first glimpse
of the lake below the rock 'towers'
but, before rushing down to it,
visit the drystone chapel, **Notre-
Dame-des-Monts** (**1h05min**).
Then descend to the refuge/
restaurant (open end June to early
September) and from here amble
round the lake. After you've
circled this sparkling blue mirror
(**1h50min**), climb the wide track

103

from the refuge, past huge stalks of summer-flowering mullein. Beyond a path off left to the Tête de Valplane, you come to a *table d'orientation* looking out towards the mountains and explaining their Alpine vegetation. But don't miss the wonderful view down to the left, where the Chadoulin Stream (a resurgence of the Lac d'Allos) threads delicate meanders through the emerald cushions of the **Plateau du Laus**, the spongy peat bog shown on page 32. The plateau was once a shallow lake, formed by the same glacier as Lake Allos.

From here you descend through larch woods *(mélèze)*. These clever conifers, 'Kings of the Alps', shed their leaves in winter, an so are less susceptible to damp and cold. Notice how gracefully they curve, as light and gravity influence their growth. Back at the FORESTRY HOUSE above the CAR PARK (**2h 35min**), you cross bedrock *(verrou)* — stone so hard that it resisted glacial erosion. Perhaps now, like us, you'll spend the rest of the day beside the meanders of the Chadoulin, while the crowds hurry past on their way to the lake.

Lac d'Allos

Walk 24: ABOVE BEUIL

Distance: 8km/5mi; 2h45min
Grade: easy-moderate, with
ascents/descents of 320m/1050ft
overall. Little shade. Yellow PR
waymarking; some short cross-
country sections (no path) are
marked with wooden sighting
posts. *IGN map 3640 OT*
Equipment: see page 61; refreshments available at Beuil
How to get there: 🚗 (Car tour 6)
or 🚌 to Beuil; park at the tourist
office on the main road (D28)
Short walk: Rétouria. 4.5km/
2.8mi; 1h25min. Easy ascent/
descent of 60m/200ft. Follow the
main walk to **Rétouria** and return
the same way.

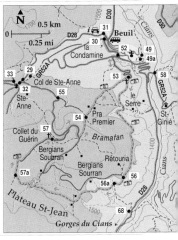

While we whizz through the eyesore of Valberg trying
not to look left or right, Beuil stops us in our tracks.
Its setting is just stunning. There are several walks around this
Alpine village, but we're convinced that this circuit shows it
off to best advantage, whatever the season.

Start out at the TOURIST OFFICE on
the main road (D28) in **Beuil**.
Walk down the road towards
GORGES DU CIANS. Some 300m/
yds downhill, at 🏁52, fork right
for CIRCUIT DE BRAMAFAN. The
cinder track soon rises in zigzags,
to a SHRINE on the right (🏁53;
15min). Continue straight ahead
at this junction, ignoring the cart
track to the right (your return
route). Rising gently on the north-
eastern flanks of the **Plateau
St-Jean**, you have fine views back
to Beuil and down left into the
Cians Valley, with the little
St-Ginié chapel on the far bank.
At a Y-fork by some buildings
(just past the shrine), keep left, on
the main track. Beyond the little
hamlet of **Le Serre** (**25min**), you
cross a stream. Beuil disappears
from view, but Les Cluots (2106m/
6907ft) in the southeast now
attracts your attention: its summit
is almost always snow-capped.
Rétouria (**45min**) is another
pretty little hamlet, with wooden-

roofed stone houses. From here
you have a good view down south
towards the Cians Gorge.
At 🏁56 you come upon another
handful of houses. Go *left* here, for
CIANS, leaving the 'Bramafan' circuit and zigzagging down towards
the road in the Cians Gorge. When
you reach 🏁56a (**55min**) some
60m/200ft downhill, turn right at
the Y-fork towards BERGIANS SOU-
BRAN. This narrow and slightly
overgrown (but well waymarked)
path gently regains the height lost,
as it rises to another group of
houses and a wooden 🏁: ITINE-
RAIRE PEDESTRE. Here you come to
a Y-fork at a BARN (**1h10min**).
Both routes are waymarked, but
take the fork to the right of the barn.
Soon the path contours above
fields, before coming into a patch
of forest and then climbing gently
through a stream bed wilderness.
At the **Fount Nouvelle** (**1h25min**)
a cart track comes in from the
right. Continue to the left of this
well on a stony path, still rising up

105

Beuil from the St-Ginié chapel on the east side of the Cians River

the stream bed. At a fork three minutes along, go right uphill, now climbing a bit more steeply. You pass to the left of a CONCRETE PLINTH (take either path at the fork here). Then walk to the left of a wooden SIGHTING POST, making for the top of the ridge ahead, where the next sighting post is visible (no waymarks).

Having risen to a crossing track, follow it to the right, to ▪57a (**1h 42min**). From here head north-east towards BERGIANS SOUBRAN, crossing a grassy PLATEAU, with a 'top of the world' feeling. Giant thistles and thousands of sheep accompany you, as well as views north to the jagged peaks of the high Mercantour. The hamlet of La Fuont is below to the right. Nearing **Bergians Soubran** you'll surely encounter goats, sheep, geese, hens, cows, horses, cats and dogs! At the **Collet du Guérin** (**1h55min**), where there is a CROSS on the left and ▪57 on the right, keep straight ahead on a lane, passing a little turning circle on the right. At a T-junction, turn right on another lane, slightly uphill. The landscape is a blanket of golden grass interwoven with strands of firs and spruce. Seven

minutes from the col, after the lane has described a wide curve to the right, watch for a SIGHTING POST on the left and go left down a wide grassy path at the left edge of the woods. It drops straight down to a grassy track and ▪54 (**2h 10min**). Go half-right here, again following the CIRCUIT DE BRAMA-FAN and passing between two cottages at **Pra Premier**. At a Y-fork, keep left downhill, straight towards Beuil. Soon the trail peters out, but just keep steeply downhill through the grassy field, towards a METAL POLE with a yellow flash. There is a beautiful view over the green valley of **La Condamine** and to Beuil. More sighting posts lead you onto a cart track descending from the right. Follow this downhill to the left, to a huge CAIRN. Continue downhill at the left of the cairn, on an old trail, with the remains of stone walls on either side. This brings you back to the SHRINE first passed at the 15min-point (**2h25min**). Turn left and retrace your outward route to **Beuil** (**2h45min**).

Walk 25: ABOVE PUGET-THENIERS

See also photographs pages 131, 133

Distance: 4.5km/2.8mi; 2h

Grade: moderate climb/descent of 330m/1100ft, but you must be sure-footed and have a head for heights. Avoid the walk in mist, strong winds and wet weather. Some of the paths cross *robines* (see page 133), where *care is needed*. Yellow PR waymarking. *IGN map 3641 OT*

Equipment: see page 61; walking stick(s). Refreshments available at Puget-Théniers

How to get there: 🚗 to the railway station at Puget-Théniers (Car tour 6), or 🚂 to Puget-Théniers (Train des Pignes; convenient departures; see page 130)

Alternative walk: Crête d'Aurafort. 12km/7.4mi; 5h. Grade as main walk, but this is strenuous, with an ascent/descent of 650m/2130ft. Start out 400m/yds west of the railway station at ◖160 on the north side of the N202. Follow the GR510 to ◖161 and ◖162. Now you begin an exhilarating scramble up the **Castagnet Cliffs** *(in full sun). Watch for the waymarks* (orange, as well as GR). Beyond ◖163, you're on the **Crête d'Aurafort** (photograph page 133), which you can follow to ◖165 — or a little further, to the Plateau de la Condamine, with its junipers, mushrooms galore, and grazing horses. Return the same way. Red/white GR waymarking

This walk is a good introduction to the *robines* of Haute-Provence. Ranging in colour from off-white to black, they have an austere beauty. Once your boots have 'got to grips' with these deeply-eroded limey-clay slopes, then return another day and do the Alternative walk. You've got to be very fit, but it is *spectacular!* Leaving the olive groves behind, you scale the sheer cliffs behind Puget-Théniers. At the top, a grassy path takes you through holm oaks to the awesome *robines* of the Crête d'Aurafort. And a bonus: *both* walks afford superb long-range views along the orchard valley of the Var.

Start out at the *RAILWAY STATION* at **Puget-Théniers**, after first calling at the superb tourist office. Walk into the village centre, then take steps at the right of the *POST OFFICE* up to the **Rue de la Redoule**. From the signpost follow a path uphill, cross the road into the cemetery, and continue to the left of the

telephone exchange (with the word JUDO on the wall!). Keep right at a fork, then *left uphill* at the next fork (where a stronger path goes straight ahead). You join a fire-fighting road, which quickly becomes a track. Before the track makes a U-bend, be sure to *turn back sharp left* uphill on the waymarked route — a centuries-old trail. Climbing in zigzags, you

enjoy fine views over Puget-Théniers and can trace the Var Valley from Utelle in the east to the castle at Entrevaux in the west. Reaching a CREST, walk (carefully) along the very top of the *robines* pouring down into the **Ravin du Planet** on your right.

Before long, the path moves away from the edge and heads west, leaving a little ruined house up above to the right. From a PASS (**1h**) you look ahead into the Roudoule Valley, backed by the Crête d'Aurafort (setting for the Alternative walk). As the walk continues uphill in tight zigzags, be sure to locate your waymarks. The **Roccia d'Abeilla** (**1h15min**) marks the top of the climb: from here there is a magnificent view east along the Var. The 'Bee's Rock' is a natural fortress, from where *robines* pour down into the Ravin du Planet. Walk on to ▶173 and, at the fork, keep straight ahead, to the ruined **Bergerie de Lava** (**1h20min**), where you can take a break on the grassy slopes. The onward walk starts from the back of the bergerie and descends to the Roudoule Valley, with views to the Crête d'Aurafort, the Castagnet Cliffs and the roofs of Puget-Théniers. This narrow path is especially beautiful in autumn, when wine-red Venetian sumac and gold grass contrasts with the dark shiny leaves of the holm oaks. Here again, *care is needed* on the *robines*. Finally the path crosses a very narrow ridge between two *robines* — this only lasts for 12m/yds, but is potentially dangerous on a windy day — and amazingly, this is when you return to 'civilisation' and are just above a house! Join the drive to the house and, where it curves to the right, turn sharp left on a cart track. When this track turns towards a house, continue down a rough, grassy trail, making for the cemetery and telephone exchange. As you approach a wooden gate, turn sharp right down a footpath. Cross a gulley on a WOODEN FOOTBRIDGE and come to the **Rue de la Roudoule** (▶175; **1h50min**). Turn left, follow the road down to ▶174, and head back to **Puget-Théniers** and the STATION (**2h**).

View west across the Roudoule Valley to the Alternative walk — the Crête d'Aurafort and the Castagnet Cliffs above Puget-Théniers

Walk 26: GRÈS D'ANNOT

See also photographs page 131
Distance: 5km/3mi; 2h15min
Grade: moderate climb/descent of
330m/1100ft, but you must be
sure-footed on the *robines* (see
page 133 and Walk 25). Avoid the
walk in mist or wet weather.
Yellow PR and dark blue triangle
waymarking. *IGN map 3541 E*
Equipment: see page 61; walking
stick(s). Refreshments available at
Annot
How to get there: 🚌 to the railway station at Annot (Car tour 6),
or 🚂 to Annot (Train des Pignes;
convenient departures; see page
130)
**Short walk/picnic suggestion:
Notre-Dame-de-Vers-la-Ville.**
25min return. From the main
square at Annot, take the street at
the right of the fountain (a build-

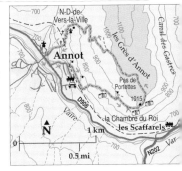

ing arches over this street, and
there is an *alimentation* on the left
and a *bar/tabac/hôtel* on the right.
Curve right into **Chemin de Vers-
la-Ville**; this becomes a lane
between fields and then zigzags up
past the 14 Stations of the Cross
to the chapel of **Notre-Dame**.

This magnificent walk, beautifully shaded by oaks and
chestnuts, takes us through a chaos of towering boulders
and rock arches, the Grès d'Annot. Midway through the hike
we skirt a cliff-face below massive rock 'totem-poles', high above
the confluence of the Vaïre and Coulomp at Les Scaffarels.

Start out at the RAILWAY STATION
at **Annot**: head downhill towards
the village, then turn right and
walk through a TUNNEL under the
railway (🚩: CIRCUIT DES GRES
D'ANNOT, CHAMBRE DU ROI). Then
turn right on a stony track, passing
the octagonal water tower for the
old steam trains. Keep along to the
last railway building (noticing the
house up to the left, built into the
first of the *grès* en route), where
the tracks disappear into a shed (🚩:
ANNOT: ESCALADE SUR LES GRES).
Just past the sign, meet a fork and
go left, climbing slightly. When
you are directly above the turn-
table for the old steam
locomotives, be sure to turn left in
the first zigzag of this stone-laid
trail (**10min**). *From now on, it is
imperative to keep watch for the
yellow waymarks.* Climb into the
rock chaos, where climbers have

inscribed mythological names on
the boulders. Paths thread out in
all directions, and *it is very easy to
lose your way here. Patiently search
out the yellow flashes.* If in doubt,
whenever possible follow paths
running parallel with the Vaïre
Valley on the right (climbing
southwest); don't head too far left.
Beyond the chaos you should find
yourself on the stone-laid trail
again (**30min**), soon crossing
some clay slopes shored up with
logs (*robines;* see page 133 and
Walk 25). Five minutes later more
shored-up *robines* are crossed and
there is a fine view to terracing on
the far side of the Vaïre.
At a crossing of paths (**50min**),
climb up to the right (🚩: CHAMBRE
DU ROI). In the shade of beautiful
chestnuts you reach the narrow
defile shown on page 131. As you
start into it, look right: ENTRÉE is

109

an overhang of rock, with a venerable chestnut in front. Now the path climbs quickly to the **Pas des Portettes**, the highest point of the walk. Turn left downhill here, passing under a high rock arch. As you descend into another rock chaos, enjoy the lovely play of light and shade, as the sun streams through the magnificent chestnuts onto the moss-covered boulders. Once in a while, the path climbs *very slightly* before descending again, but *be sure not to climb too far up to the right*. Some seven-eight minutes below the pass, watch for tree limbs across the path, or you will miss your turn-off: you must go *sharp left* downhill. (If you find yourself walking north above Annot, you've gone too far.) Always watch for branches across the path, and *at every fork, take the time to look for a* DARK BLUE TRIANGLE *waymark*. About 15 minutes down from the pass (**1h35min**) the path becomes so narrow that you may think you're lost (the yellow flashes are *very* sparse on this stretch), but keep ahead across some mucky streams, soon accompanied by the pleasant sound of running water. You pass a building on the left dated 1672 and two minutes later come to the 12th-century chapel of **Notre-Dame-de-Vers-la-Ville** on the left (**1h55min**). Its wall-belfry is surmounted by a stone cross. From here a grassy stone-laid trail takes you downhill in zigzags, past the **14 Stations of the Cross**, each embellished with a naïve painting on glazed tiles. Cross the RAILWAY and follow a lane between colourful gardens and fields. When you come into **Annot**, head left on the main road. Turn left for GARE to get back to the STATION (**2h15min**).

written in red on a stone. If you're slim enough, and not claustrophobic, squat down and crawl through this opening, into the three huge rock 'rooms', illuminated by a small gap high above. Then return and continue through the towering, shady defile. At the end of the passage you come to a CLEARING with a fireplace and boulder-benches — a lovely picnic spot. The path continues up to the cliff-edge, from where there is a breath-taking view down over the apron of emerald cultivation skirting the confluence of roads and streams at Les Scaffarels. Now a fabulous 'balcony' path (amply wide, but watch your footing and *take special care* on windy days) carries you east in the setting shown above (**1h05min**). Once round the bluff, you head inland through chestnuts and pine. If you start to lose the way as the path climbs over bed-rock, look ahead to see footholds cut into the rock. Beyond the bed-rock the clear path climbs gently through a mossy glen, full of ferns and tall trees embraced by ivy. You pass to the right of a STONE SHELTER (**1h20min**) built below

Walk 27: AIGLUN AND THE ESTERON RIVER

Distance: 7.5km/4.7mi; 2h50min
Grade: moderate descent/ascent of 170m/560ft, but you must be sure-footed and agile for the initial descent. Yellow PR, red and white GR waymarking. *IGN map 3542 ET*
Equipment: see page 61; walking stick(s). Refreshments available at Aiglun
How to get there: 🚗 (Car tour 7) or 🚌 to Aiglun
Note: There used to be a path on the south side of the Esteron from the Pont de Végay to the suspen-

sion bridge shown below (below Vascognes). At time of writing this path was closed because of a landslip, but the suspension bridge was still open. If, when you reach the Pont de Végay (☞85), there is a signpost directing you *ahead along the river* to Vascognes, take that route. When you come to the suspension bridge (☞86), cross it and, in Vascognes, turn right on the lane, to pick up the main walk at the 1h25min-point. Times are unaffected.

This circuit through pleasant oak woods in the Esteron Valley offers some fine views to the perched villages of Aiglun and Sigale — as well as a textbook introduction to Mediterranean fungi! But the bounding Esteron will be, without doubt, the focus of your attention.

Start out in **Aiglun** at the MAIRIE: from ☞81 descend paved steps and then a narrow, very stony path marked with yellow flashes. Below, you can see a bridge over the Esteron. Your path goes *straight* down to it, crossing an old lane and then a track. It's very steep; sometimes you'll be scrambling on all fours. When you drop down to this lovely old STONE BRIDGE (**25min**), cross it and, on the far side, turn left on a track. In a minute you pass ☞82, where you join the GR4 and cross a tributary a minute later. Now look back to Aiglun, strung out between the walls of its *clue* and the cemetery chapel of Notre-Dame. In autumn, colonies of

View back to Aiglun from the Esteron Valley (top) and the Pont de Vascognes (right), which can still be crossed (see 'Note' above)

View east along the Esteron (top) and olive groves below Sigale

(**1h25min**). Continue on the lane to the D10 (**1h40min**) and turn left. Pass a SHRINE on the right and, just beyond it, turn right up a concrete lane (⌐87). Quickly coming to wrought-iron gates, you meet a fork: go left just *before* the gates, following a footpath. At a Y-fork almost imediately, go right on a grassy path. All the climbing to regain height is done on this pretty, shady path, through oaks and broom. It is narrow but very well waymarked; follow the waymarks *carefully,* so as not to miss any U-turns.

Passing under the rock needles of the **Bau du Bouquet**, the climb levels out (**2h10min**), and there are more views back down the valley to Sigale. It's a pity to leave the birdsong of this bower, but soon the path deposits you on the D10 again, at ⌐88 (**2h35min**). Turn right and follow the road for 1km, back to **Aiglun** (**2h50min**). There's another fine view to the Végay falls as you pass below Notre-Dame.

utterly revolting, slimy black fungi sprout along this track; our French textbook assures us that they are *coprin à chevelure* and edible!

At ⌐83 (**35min**) continue ahead for PONT DE VEGAY. About eight minutes later there is a view to the Cascade de Végay (not on the map) from a signpost indicating a path up to the falls. Ignore the sign; continue ahead past a lovely rock pool. Around here the diagonal strata in the orange cliffs draw your attention — as does Sigale, straddling the cliffs up ahead, beyond the Riolan Gorge. At the **Pont de Végay** (⌐85; **1h 05min**, turn left and cross the bridge. Turn right on the little lane on the far side and follow it for a little over 1km, to **Vascognes**

Right: the Lac de Castillon (Walk 28 and Car tours 5 and 7). During Car tour 5 you skirt the full length of this huge man-made lake, a mirror of sparkling reflections. Notice the folds of beige earth streaming down the slopes; these are robines, *outpourings of crumbly, limey-clay soil. They are prevalent throughout Alpes de Haute-Provence; we call them 'elephants', and you'll soon realise why! Walks 25 and 26 cross many* robines.

Walk 28: VILLE

Distance: 2.5km/1.5mi; 50min
Grade: very easy. No waymarking. *IGN map 3542 OT*
Equipment: stout shoes; refreshments available in Demandolx
How to get there: 🚗 to the U-bend of the C2 just 2km west of Demandolx (Car tour 7). Park at the side of the track (the track may be blocked off with boulders).

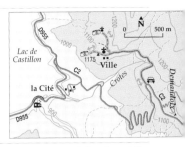

This stroll to the ruined hamlet of Ville, and the short hike up to the chapel beyond it, afford incredibly beautiful views over the turquoise Lac de Castillon, edged by beige *robines* and lush green alpine slopes.

Start out on the C2: follow the track, below beautifully-striated cliffs, to the ruins of **Ville** (**15min**). Just past the end of the track, *before* the first house of the hamlet, the footpath on the right will be your ongoing route. After exploring the ruins, walk out to the grassy promontory beyond them for breathtaking views of the lake and dam. Then go back to the path passed earlier and turn left uphill; vague at first, it quickly becomes well defined. Three-four minutes up, go right at a fork. Rise past a tall stone CAIRN/SHRINE and walk on through globe thistles, box and pines — to a CHAPEL on a grassy knoll (**30min**), from where the views are even more extensive. You *may* see some tall Disney-like structures on the hillside opposite, at Blaron; we call them the 'Three Kings'. Erected by a religious sect, they have been a thorn in the side of Castellane Council for years and, according to the newspapers, are finally to be dismantled. From here retrace your steps to the C2 (**50min**).

Walk 29: CIRCUIT AROUND COMPS-SUR-ARTUBY

See photograph pages 40-41
Distance: 3km/2mi; 1h10min
Grade: easy ascent/descent of about 100m/330ft. Green and white, some blue and yellow PR waymarking. *IGN map 3543 OT*
Equipment: see page 61; stout shoes will suffice. Refreshments available at Comps
How to get there: 🚗 to Comps (Car tour 7), then go right on the D21 towards LA SOUCHE. But 2.2km along, where the D221 goes left to La Souche, turn right to a picnic area by a factory.
Hint: Go left on the D221; just past La Souche there is a lovely Roman bridge over the Artuby.

This very short walk, an ideal leg-stretcher, visits a delightful chapel and a 13th-century Gothic church, from where you can survey the beautiful green fields around Comps and look out to the mountains edging the Gorges du Verdon.

Start out at the PICNIC AREA: walk south along the lane, with the FACTORY on the right and a RIVER POOL on the left. Just 1m/yd *before* two PILLARS on the lane, climb the green/white-waymarked path on the right. This grassy path, sometimes shaded by pines, rises between bluffs, above the **Artuby River**. Some 400m/yds uphill, just *past* a white 'change of direction' waymark, be sure to turn uphill to the right at a huge CAIRN (where another path runs straight ahead). Soon the path levels out, and Comps is visible ahead. To the left, on the far side of the Artuby Gorge, is the little Notre-Dame chapel that makes such a lovely picnic spot on Car tour 7. When a cart track comes in from the left behind you, join it and continue ahead. Before the track becomes tarred, turn right up steps, to the **Chapelle St-Jean** (**25min**). Now follow the crest behind the chapel, take in the views (including Robion in the north and the twin ruined towers of Bargème in the

near northeast), before walking on to the 13th-century Gothic church of **St-André** (**35min**), with its beautifully-made water tank. From here take the walkway down through Comps, to the D955. Then turn right on the lane adjacent to the MAIRIE/POSTE (the *boulangerie* will be on your left). Ignore a track off to the left 100m/yds along. 60m/yds further on, turn right downhill (YELLOW/BLUE WAYMARKS on a pylon), into another mini-gorge. The way becomes a path and emerges in a grassy area at the left-hand edge of conifers. Do *not* head down left into the valley here: keep contouring, so that you soon have conifers on both sides. Watch for an open-sided storage shed ahead, below you; your path runs to the left of it, *just to the left of the factory fence* (which soon becomes visible). Once you pass the barn, the path descends a bit more steeply *and crosses a ditch*. Turn right on a track on the far side of the ditch, back to the PICNIC AREA (**1h10min**).

Walk 30: ABOVE TOURTOUR

Distance: 7.5km/4.7mi; 1h55min
Grade: easy, with ascents/descents of 120m/400ft overall; little shade. No consistent waymarking, but easily followed. *IGN map 3443 OT*
Equipment: see page 61; stout shoes will suffice. Refreshments available at Tourtour
How to get there: 🚗 to Tourtour (Car tour 7), or 🚌 to Tourtour
Short walk: Moulières. 3.5km/ 2.2mi; 55min. Easy; access by 🚗. There is a large parking area beside FIRE TRACK K45 at **Moulières** (see map). Start and end the walk there, perhaps visiting the Tour de Grimaldi as well.
Alternative walk: Tour de Grimaldi. 9km/5.6mi; 2h25min. From the 17min-point in the main walk, make a detour to the Tour de Grimaldi (on a lane).

The hamlets of Moulières — old and new — are the focal points of this walk, but you will also enjoy fine views back to Tourtour and ahead to the Maures and Esterel, as you cross a textbook example of *garrigues*. The walk is best done in spring, when the limestone-loving vegetation is in full flower.

Start out at the multi-spouted FOUNTAIN in the main square in **Tourtour**: follow the **Rue du Lavoir** (a small sign indicates TOUR DE GRIMALDI). You climb north past a fort on the left and the old — but still used — washing place (*lavoir*) on the right. Further to the right are verdant fields. Fork left in front of a large IRON CROSS and a tiny CHAPEL (**6min**). At a junction six minutes later, go straight across towards the houses. Ignore the lane off left to the Grimaldi Tower (**17min**). *(The Alternative walk heads left here, for a half-hour detour.)* Cross a STREAM (**25min**) in the latter-day hamlet of **Moulières**, where the rustic houses, poplar woods, and splendid vegetable and flower gardens are a delight. Pass FIRE TRACK K45 off to the right (your return route and parking for the Short walk). Almost immediately, just in front of an electricity PYLON, you come to a three-way junction (**30min**): curve right with the main track, pass a drive off left to a house and, 40 paces futher on, turn right on FIRE TRACK K66, through a stand of cypresses. Ignore a track off to the right after 30 paces. Now climb above the valley on a stony track. Seven

minutes along, go straight over a crossing track, to pass to the left of the summit of **Camp Redon**. Aups is visible in the distance now, to the right of a quarry.
When the track that passed to the east of Redon comes in from behind and to the right, continue left downhill under the welcome shade of pines. Below a rocky crag up on your left, you come to a fork. Turn right on FIRE TRACK K45 (K66 continues ahead) and, at the next fork, go right again. You

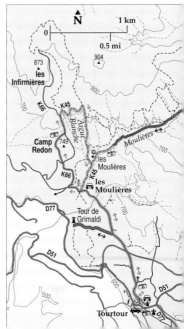

Tourtour from the Rue du Lavoir (top), poplar wood near fire track K45 at Moulières (middle), and the old mill beside the watercourse

cross the **Aigue Blanche** stream bed (**55min**) and come to a T-junction. Turn right here. Two minutes later, ignore a track off to the left; keep ahead on a narrower

trail, straight towards the poplars at Moulières. Six minutes after that, ignore another track off left (although it has yellow flash waymarks). But four minutes later, at a Y-fork, *do turn left:* curl steeply downhill to another track, passing huge ancient oaks on the right. You've entered a grotto just behind the poplar wood, and a watercourse (sadly dry for the last couple of years) is on your right. At another fork, a couple of minutes along, again go left — to the ruins of the old hamlet and mill of **Moulières** (**1h15min**). Pause a while in this gorgeous ferny glen, where light and shade play over the ruins and contorted rocks beside the stream. (Since this is a very short walk, you may like to continue for a while beside the watercourse on the gorgeous grassy path in this mini-gorge, the **Vallon des Moulières**.)

Then return the same way, but keep left at the first fork, to follow FIRE TRACK K45 back to **Moulières** (**1h20min**). Then turn left and retrace your steps to **Tourtour** (**1h55min**).

Walk 31: SENTIER MARTEL

See also photos pages 44-47
Distance: 14km/8.7mi; 6h
Grade: moderate-strenuous, with 450m/1475ft and 350m/1150ft of ascent overall. Two tunnels en route, one of them 700m/0.4mi long. The initial descent is steep, and there is a further descent at the Brèche Imbert, down a metal 'staircase' (250 steps; see photograph overleaf), where you must be sure-footed and have a head for heights. Red and white GR waymarking. *IGN map 3442 OT*
Note: *Remember that the Verdon supplies a battery of factories and hydroelectric stations; it is dangerous to venture too far off the riverbank; the water can rise very suddenly without warning.*
Equipment: see page 61; *torch, plenty of water,* warm clothing. Refreshments available at La Maline and Point Sublime
How to get there: 🚌 to Point Sublime (Car tour 8). Here you will find taxis (or can telephone for a taxi). The taxi driver will ask you to move your car to the Samson Corridor, from where he will take you 18km west to the Chalet de la Maline, where the walk starts. (If you leave your car at Point Sublime, you must climb an additional 150m/500ft.) Alternatively, do the walk with friends, and leave a car either end. *Leave nothing of value in your car.*

Short walk: Baume aux Pigeons. 3km/2mi; 1h. Easy, but you need a *torch*). Park at the **Samson Corridor**: the road (D236) is under 1km east of the inn at Point Sublime (Car tour 8). From the PARKING BAY at the end of this road, follow the GR4 (red and white waymarks) as far as the steps in the tunnel, descend (if you like) to the river, and return the same way. *Very crowded on weekends and in the summer.*

Alternative walk: Brèche Imbert. 12km/7.5mi; 5h30min. Moderate; access/equipment as for the Short walk. Follow the GR4 as far as the metal staircase at the Brèche Imbert; return the same way.

This is *the* classic itinerary in Provence, and arguably the most beautiful (and crowded) walk in all Europe. At the height of the season, more than 2500 people *a day* pass through the Samson Corridor. *Please* try to go in spring or autumn, mid-week, on a clear, crisp day. You have an unforgettable experience in store, and it's worth waiting for perfect weather conditions.

Start out facing the **Chalet de la Maline**: take the GR4 footpath at the northeast side of the building. After rounding a ravine, the path descends from the **Pas d'Issane** in hairpins *(keep to the zigzags, to prevent further erosion)*. Dropping to a junction, turn left on the **Sentier Martel (50min)**. E-A Martel (see Car tour 8, page 43) was the first person to explore the depths of the gorge, in 1905 — commissioned by the company who planned to built a 25km-long watercourse from Carejuan to Galetas. The project was abandoned during World War I, but is the reason for all the tunnels and screes along the route. A few more zigzags take you to a 'balcony' path 10m/30ft above the river. Look up across the canyon to the Auberge des Cavaliers atop the cliff. Now follow the right bank of the river upstream. You might miss the **Pré d'Issane**, some 30 minutes along, but there is evidence that man cultivated this river bank meadow even in prehistoric times.
The path then climbs to the

117

The dramatic descent at the Brèche Imbert

Guègues scree, which is crossed via metal stairs with a handrail. A little over 10 minutes beyond here, watch for the **Baume aux Bœufs**, a huge vault in the rock (named for the cow bones found here many years ago). Ten minutes later, at a junction where the Sentier Martel continues to the left, go *right*. In under 15 minutes

you're at **La Mescla (2h20min)**, the setting shown on pages 46-47, where the canyon of the Artuby comes in from the south and the Verdon describes a tight meander. This is the halfway point in the walk and an area of indescribable beauty. It's easy to get down to the gravelly river bed, but *do not* attempt to swim here — the currents are treacherous. Returning from La Mescla, head right at the T-junction, climbing steeply to the **Brèche Imbert (3h)**, named for the engineer who opened this crevice for walkers. As you look straight down 120m/

400ft to the river below, *descend the metal staircase slowly and carefully*. Once back down on *terra firma*, you climb below the **Baume aux Hirondelles** and then descend in a U-turn, to pass below the **Baume aux Chiens**. After meeting the river at the **Plage des Fères**, you climb again below the steep orange cliffs of the **Escalès**, rising 500m/1650ft above you (photograph page 44). You may spot climbers on the really sheer part of these cliffs, further east. After passing to the right of a first TUNNEL (disused and dangerous), you enter the **Samson Corridor**.

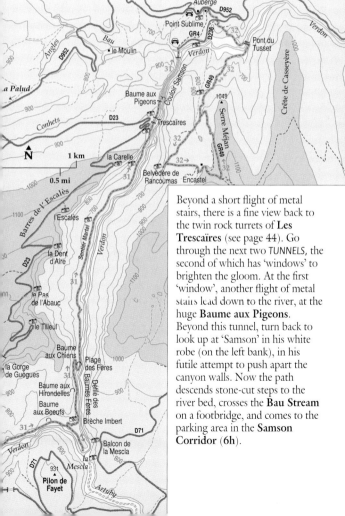

Beyond a short flight of metal stairs, there is a fine view back to the twin rock turrets of **Les Trescaïres** (see page 44). Go through the next two TUNNELS, the second of which has 'windows' to brighten the gloom. At the first 'window', another flight of metal stairs lead down to the river, at the huge **Baume aux Pigeons**. Beyond this tunnel, turn back to look up at 'Samson' in his white robe (on the left bank), in his futile attempt to push apart the canyon walls. Now the path descends stone-cut steps to the river bed, crosses the **Bau Stream** on a footbridge, and comes to the parking area in the **Samson Corridor (6h)**.

Walk 32: BELVEDERE DE RANCOUMAS

See map pages 118-119, see also photographs page 44
Distance: 8km/5mi; 3h30min
Grade: fairly strenuous ascents/descents of 600m/2000ft overall. Good, shady paths. Red and white GR, sparse yellow PR waymarking. One pathless section requires a good sense of direction. *IGN map 3442 OT*
Equipment: see page 61; warm clothing in cold weather. There is a spring (sometimes dry) at the 50min-point; refreshments available at Point Sublime
How to get there: 🚐 to the car park at Point Sublime (Car tour 8). *Leave nothing in your car.*
Short walk: Pont du Tusset. 2km/1.2mi; under 1h. Easy descent/ascent of 200m/650ft; stout shoes will suffice. Follow the main walk for 25min and return the same way.

T wo gorgeous, but little frequented beauty spots in the Verdon are the highlights of this walk — the old Roman bridge below Point Sublime and an emerald eyrie opposite the Escalès climbing edge, with plunging views into the gorge.

Start out at the inn at **Point Sublime**: walk downhill towards CAREJUAN. After 100m, just in front of an INFORMATION PANEL about the Sentier Martel (Walk 31), turn right down a footpath, following the red and white waymarks of the GR4 and GR49. At a fork in three minutes, go left with the GR49 (the GR4 goes right to the Samson Corridor). At a Y-fork almost immediately, bear right downhill. Cross the access road to the Samson Corridor and follow the stony track ahead (☛: SENTIER D'ENCASTEL). At a junction, ignore the path to the right (marked with a red and white 'X'); turn left down a narrow path through mixed oaks sprinkled with conifers (☛: GR49). Soon you hear the sound of rushing water. Three minutes past the junction, ignore a path to the left (also marked with an 'X').
After a descent of 200m/650ft, you're on the 2000-year-old **Pont du Tusset** (**25min**), crossing the roaring turquoise river. Just beyond the bridge, curve uphill to the right (*part of the path is broken away here; watch your step*). Some Montpellier maples grace the path, together with the Venetian sumac shown opposite. You pass a SPRING on your left (**50min**); if it's not dry, its gurgling will alert you to it. Further up, when you are level with the viewpoint at Point Sublime, there are fine views over to the village of Rougon. Some 15 minutes past the spring, begin climbing in zigzags. At a fork where the GR49 curls up to the left in a U-turn (**1h20min**; our return route); keep *right* on a good, but narrow path, where you may notice some faded yellow waymarks. (Don't confuse the forestry signs here with GR flashes; see the notes on page 63.) A stream is crossed about five minutes past the fork. Beyond the stream, bear left uphill at a Y-fork. The walk soon levels out, and you're on a high PLATEAU (**1h 30min**), deep in the golden grasses of abandoned terraces, now invaded by junipers and wild roses. Keep heading in the same direction, with the walls of the canyon on your right, and soon you will spot a patch of emerald green ahead. Just before you get there, notice the path joining you from the left; it is marked with cairns and faded yellow waymarks; this is your ongoing route.
The grassy **Belvédère de Rancoumas** (**1h40min**) is a sun-trap and a perfect picnic spot. The canyon

walls fall 400m/1300ft below you here. Can you bear to look over the edge? Opposite, to the left, is the (100m/300ft higher) climbing wall of the **Escalès** on the north bank (photograph page 44), with the Sentier Martel below it; to the right you can spot the railings at the Belvédère des Trescaïres; these twin turrets, shown on page 44, are below you to the right.

From the viewpoint head east along the path passed earlier, through a splurge of broom, lavender, heather and pines. Coming over a small rise, you see the old hamlet of **Encastel** ahead, surrounded by green pastures. Skip down to it and pass to the *right* of the house that is intact and to the left of the ruins, on a level grassy trail. *Now take care, as there are no waymarks.* When the trail reduces to a barely-perceptible path (and you have lost sight of the ruins because of foliage), *keep more or less on a level contour, while moving slightly to the left* (don't climb up right or *descend* to the

The Pont du Tusset. In autumn Venetian sumach (Cotinus coggygria), prized for flower arrangements, lights up all the slopes in Haute-Provence

left). Going through more abandoned terraces, you pass a WATERING HOLE, come into woodland, and meet a strong crossing path on a bend (**2h**). Follow this lovely woodland path (GR49) down to the fork first encountered at the 1h20min-point in the walk. Turn down right here, in the hairpin bend, and retrace your outgoing route. Take on water at the SPRING; it's a tiring climb back up to **Point Sublime** (**3h30min**).

As you look towards the north bank from the Belvédère de Rancoumas, the canyon walls are so close together that it's hard to believe there's a 400m drop to the river between them!

Walk 33: CHARTREUSE DE LA VERNE

Chartreuse de la Verne

Distance: 5km/3mi; 1h35min
Grade: easy ascent/descent of
about 130m/425ft overall. Little
shade. Blue, then yellow PR waymarking. *IGN map 3545 OT*
Equipment: see page 61; refreshments at Collobrières, Grimaud
How to get there: 🚗 to the Chartreuse de la Verne (Car tour 9).
Open 10am-5pm except Tue.
Closed Nov, 25 Dec, Easter.

E arly October is a good time to visit the Chartreuse, if only
to enjoy the antics of the local chestnut-gatherers. This
walk gives a fine variety of views, especially over to the sea
and the Gulf of St-Tropez.

Start out at the **Chartreuse de la
Verne**. Walk past the south front
(shown above). At the fork that
follows immediately, take the
upper route to the right, rising
through a beautiful sweet chestnut
wood on a lane. Despite all the
notices prohibiting the taking of
chestnuts, in autumn the locals
will be gathered en masse to
collect them, with large tables for
sorting — and, later, picnicking.
Pass a SPRING on the right (**7min**).
Just as the lane makes a U-turn to
the right, keep left on a track (faded
BLUE FLASHES on rocks underfoot).
Almost immediately you have a
brilliant view over a reservoir and
the Gulf of St-Tropez. The chestnuts have given way to holm oaks
and *garrigues;* there are fine, open
views. After crossing a second
stream, you look north-northeast
towards white crystalline rocks on
the highest ridge in the Maures
(the Roches Blanches), with the
mountains of Haute-Provence
behind them, and northeast to

Grimaud with its twin towers,
backed by the Rocher de Roquebrune and the Esterel.
At a junction of FIRE TRACKS
(**35min**), you pass a turn-off left
near the summit of **L'Argentière**.
Ignore the 'Noyer' track to the
left; keep ahead on SIVADIERES,
passing the **Refuge des Sivadières**
on the right, in a pretty grove of
oaks. Strawberry trees and heather
line this stretch, while vineyards
edge the N98 below on the left.
At a Y-junction below the **Sommet
du Péra** (**55min**), turn sharp right
on a tarred lane (⌐: ROUTE DE LA
CRETE, now rounding the west side
of **L'Ermitage**. The relay at
Notre-Dame-des-Anges can be
seen to the left, with the Montagne Sainte-Victoire behind it.
At the following junction there is a
CISTERN on the left; walk ahead to
a 'no entry' sign with a YELLOW
FLASH and take the footpath behind
it. This leads through more chestnut woods, back to the **Chartreuse
de la Verne** (**1h35min**).

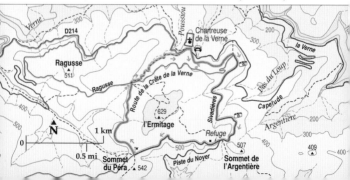

Walk 34: CAP LARDIER

Distance: 8km/5mi; 3h
Grade: fairly easy-moderate, with ascents/descents of 250m/820ft overall. Some agility is required. The walk is very exposed to sun *and wind*. Yellow PR waymarking. *IGN map 3545 OT*
Equipment: see page 61; swimming things, ample sun protection. Refreshments available at Gigaro
How to get there: 🚌 to Gigaro (detour on Car tour 9). From the

D93 between Ramatuelle and La Croix-Valmer, follow signposting for *GIGARO* (VC154). Once on the coast, drive along the esplanade and park where the road turns inland.
Short walk: Les Pins Blancs. 5.5km/3.4mi; 2h05min. Fairly easy. Follow the main walk for 55min, then either return the same way or take the inland route by picking up the main walk from the 2h05min-point.

This coastal walk is really amazing. If you wish, and if you can arrange transport, you can follow the shore with very few interruptions all the way to the centre of St-Tropez. It's almost too good to be true that some 30km of pristine coast-line has been saved from development and is currently a conservation area. You will pass gorgeous beaches, picnic amidst a bouquet of wild flowers, and enjoy refreshing sea breezes.

Start out in **Gigaro**, just where the road skirting the esplanade turns inland. Here you pick up the coastal footpath (🏃: *SENTIER LITTORAL*). The information panel here shows various routes in the area and estimated walking times; our route is waymarked in yellow. Follow the sandy path under the shade of false acacias. As soon as you leave the main part of Gigaro's beach, you will see very few people taking advantage of the isolated coves, each with its own tiny sandy beach, set apart from the others by fingers of rock. Yellow-flowering sneezewort *(Achillea)* grows all along the cliff here. Having crossed a creek, you come to a lovely group of umbrella pines, **Les Pins Parasols** (**15min**). This is just one of many idyllic settings for a picnic. Beyond the **Plage de Jovat** (**25min**) the way divides, and a green-waymarked footpath, the Sentier du Brouis, climbs inland. Keep right, along the beach. Five minutes later you pass a beach hut, the **Cabanon du Pêcheur**. Not long after, you reach the **Pointe du Brouis**. Beyond here the path is less 'tame', and there are few

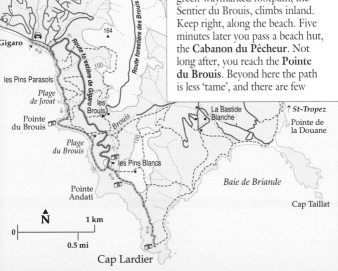

people about. Now you descend towards the beach through thistles and grasses — in early summer, this path is a medley of lavender- and gold-flowering plants. Passing behind the **Plage du Brouis** (**45min**), head right when you come to a fork (don't go left up into the umbrella pines). This takes you to a major, signposted junction, where Gigaro is back to the left. Go right here (☞: *CAP LARDIER*), ploughing through the sand, then quickly regaining the earthen path, which is so much easier underfoot. Now a steep climb (sometimes a scramble, where you will need to use your hands) takes you up to a *PASS* where there is a track and a few tall umbrella pines (**Les Pins Blancs**; **55min**).

Turn right through a sea of purple thistles and gold grasses. In a minute you come to another sign-post: to the left a path waymarked in green climbs a conical hill to a ruined forestry house (La Bastide Blanche). Our route is to the right (☞: *CAP LARDIER, CAP TAILLAT*). Head right, under kermes oaks. The path levels out as you look down on a gorgeous turquoise sea. Butterflies abound here, as does white-flowering Montpellier cistus and the red-berried mastic bush (*Pistacia lentiscus*). The route descends gently, joining a track coming in from the left.

From the old BATTERY at **Cap Lardier** (**1h30min**) the path continues east to Cap Taillat and St-Tropez. But climb back the way you came and, just beyond the signpost for Cap Lardier (at Les Pins Blancs; **2h05min**), fork right (☞: *GIGARO PAR L'INTERIEUR*). Almost immediately, fork right again (☞: *PISTE FORESTIERE PRINCIPALE*). Soon this wide track curves round to give lovely views over the sea again, and down to the coastal path. Over on the right is one of the most beautiful forests of umbrella pines you'll ever see — the hillside is a pin-cushion of emerald-green velvet, padded with the gentle mounds of these luminous, soft-needled trees. Twenty minutes along the track, you could head back to the sea for a swim, when you pass a left turn down to the Plage du Brouis. Or continue on the sun-baked track, through cork oaks and large quaking grass — *Briza maxima*, easily recognised by its shrimp-shaped head. Beyond the information panels, return to your car at **Gigaro** (**3h**).

Parasol pines and cooling sea breezes add to the exhilaration of this coastal walk. Remember that the breeze can be deceptively cooling; always take a cover-up to protect yourself from the sun!

Walk 35: LA MONTAGNE STE-VICTOIRE

**See map pages 128-129; see also
photographs pages 4-5, 59
Distance:** 11km/6.8mi; 4h
Grade: strenuous, with an ascent/
descent of 600m/1970ft. The trails
and paths are *extremely stony* underfoot. *Allow plenty of time (at least
6h) for this walk, especially in hot
weather. The descent over loose stones
takes almost as long as the climb.* The
walk is best begun early in the
morning on a cool, *but not windy*
day. Red and white GR waymarking. *IGN map 3244 ET*
Note: Prone to forest fires, the Ste-
Victoire massif may be closed to
walkers from July to September.
Ask in advance at a nearby *mairie.*
Equipment: see page 61; walking
stick(s), warm clothing in cold
weather. Allow *two litres of water
per person* (there are no springs en
route and, at time of writing, the
well at the chapel is not working).
Refreshments available at Vauvenargues (2km)
How to get there: 🚌 to Les
Cabassols, 2km west of Vauvenargues on the D10 (Car tour
10); park at the parking area by
the bus shelter. Or 🚐 to Les
Cabassols

O ne of the most famous hikes in the South of France, the
ascent of Ste-Victoire is a 'must'. We have taken the
classic route, which follows the GR9 up the north side of the
mountain. *Technically* the walk is easy. But this is a brutal
mountain— sun-baked, wind-blasted, stony and hostile.
Choose your day carefully! Ideally you want to be walking on
a clear but still, cool day between October and early May.

Start out at the BUS SHELTER at
Les Cabassols. Follow a path
heading left (east) out of the
parking area (⬆: PRIEURE DE STE-
VICTOIRE). The path, with red and
white GR waymarks, takes you
downhill — disheartening, since
you know it will only add to the
total ascent! At a fork met immediately, bear right. At the next
fork, again go right, down a stony
path. You cross a STREAM (**5min**).
Just beyond it, at another fork,
again go right downhill. Then fork
right for a fourth time, rounding a
METAL GATE. The hamlet of Les
Cabassols is left behind, and you
finally begin the ascent (**10min**).
At any fork watch for GR waymarks — particularly 15 minutes
uphill, where paths go either side
of a kermes oak grove: keep right.
The first notable LANDMARK on
this tedious uphill slog comes up
when the trail forks round either
side of pine trees twice in succession (**55min**). (Climbing in hot
weather, we reached this point in
1h10min *including stops,* and it
took us 2h30min to get to the
chapel, so these trees are a good
indication of how long it will take
you to get to the top.)
After about an hour, you may be
amazed at how much ground
you've covered; while the chapel is
still a long way off, at least it now
seems within reach. The Pic des
Mouches, the highest summit on
Ste-Victoire (1011m/ 3316ft) is
seen rising on the far left.
The stony trail ends at spot height
722m, where there is a METAL SEAT
(**1h25min**). Take a break here,
before continuing straight uphill
on a narrow footpath. By the time
the path begins to climb in
zigzags, you will be above the tree-
line, crossing *garrigues.* The sun
can be brutal now, but at least the
deep hairpin bends take the strain
off the lungs. Do watch for the
waymarks here, being sure to turn
sharply into the zigzags. (There
are many short-cuts off these
hairpin bends; *please don't use*

them: they cost too much energy *and* they erode the main path.) Eventually the lovely valley at Vauvenargues is seen below (**1h45min**), and there is a fine view west over the tail of the turquoise-blue Bimont Reservoir. As you near the summit, in a shower of wild flowers, notice that the limestone mule trail is worn to a white-marble shine by centuries of footfalls. Just beyond another metal bench surrounded by irises and daisies, you reach the 17th-century chapel shown below, the **Prieuré Notre-Dame** (**2h10min**).

It is set in a limestone cradle, with a cross rising on a rocky spit 60m/200ft above it. Nearby is a simple refuge, completely bare except perhaps for a pile of wood. There is also a well here but, at time of writing, it was not working.

From the refuge walk towards the rock cutting on the south side of the mountain, *taking care to avoid the huge pit behind the pine tree.* As soon as you reach this colossal **Brèche des Moines** (Monks' Gap), you will probably sink to your knees like everyone else, as the abyss below you is revealed. Now you will see why we chose the northern ascent; the paths coming up from the south are difficult and vertiginous.

No doubt you will want to

Left: the Prieuré Notre-Dame, with the Croix de Provence behind it. The Brèche des Moines is the cutting to the right, below the cross. Below: Ste-Victoire from the D17, with the Croix de Provence clearly visible. The paths that ascend the mountain from this south side are much more demanding than the GR9.

continue up to the cross — the beacon that rises over all the walks and tours around the mountain. The scramble up to it requires agility and, while it's not difficult, the boot-polished rocks are very slippery. However, coming back down, it is easy to miss the main path, in which case you could find yourself on a very awkward and vertiginous scree slope. So *pay close attention to the path you take up to the cross.*

Clamber up to the **Croix de Provence** (**2h20min**). It's certainly worth the effort, because there is a tiny METAL HUT cum viewing platform up here. Those of us who suffer from vertigo can stand in the protection of its walls and look straight down the south side of the mountain, where the bright limestone cliffs are embedded in vivid red clay. Here the Ste-Baume massif rises beyond the valley of the Arc to the southeast. The Barrage de Bimont glimmers in the northwest, where the Lubéron drops down to the Durance. In the east, beyond the Pic des Mouches, the Provençal Alps seem a hazy mirage. Dedicated on 18 May 1875 (and restored in 1983), the massive cross is strung with lights. It's hard to imagine how anyone could have put them there or, indeed, how such a huge structure was raised in this vertiginous spot, some 30m/100ft above the mountain spine. Having returned to the chapel (sometimes on all fours), descend overlooking the Bimont Reservoir and the Cause Valley. Unfortunately, this descent on *very* loose stones is even more tiring than the ascent. Back at the SEAT at spot height 722m (**3h**), the path becomes a trail. At the fork by the kermes oak grove (first passed 15 minutes uphill) be sure to go left. After crossing the stream, you rise back to **Les Cabassols** (**4h**).

Walk 36: LAC ZOLA

See also photograph page 60
Distance: 6.5km/4mi; 2h10min
Grade: fairly easy, with ascents/descents of 250m/820ft overall. Good, if rather stony, tracks and paths underfoot. Varied waymarking colours. *IGN map 3244 ET*
Note: Prone to forest fires, the Ste-Victoire massif may be closed to walkers from July to September. Ask in advance at a nearby *mairie*.
Equipment: see page 61; swimming things. Refreshments available at Aix-en-Provence (6km)
How to get there: 🚌 to Le Tholonet (park in the parking area opposite the château; Car tour 10), or 🚌 to Le Tholonet
Alternative walks
1 **Aqueduc de Doudon.** 8km/5mi; 2h45min. Ascents/descents of 300m/1000ft overall. Follow the main walk for 1h, then continue ahead along the track, to the AQUEDUCT that carries water from the Bimont Reservoir to the plains south of Aix. Turn left here and, at a crossing track with GREEN WAYMARKS, turn left again. Rejoining the main walk south of **Lac Zola**, follow it to the end.
2 **Lac de Bimont.** 12.5km/7.8mi; 4h. Ascents/descents of 350m/1150ft overall. Do Alternative walk 1 above, but, when you meet the track waymarked in green, keep right. Continue on a track with RED WAYMARKS, to the DAM at the **Lac de Bimont.** Return the same way, then turn right on the track with GREEN WAYMARKS, to get to **Lac Zola.** Rejoin the main walk at the 1h25min-point. *Alternatively, cross* the **Bimont** DAM and take the path with YELLOW WAYMARKS to Lac Zola.

This delightful hike takes you to a very pretty small lake, with pleasant views to the cross atop Ste-Victoire. On the way we make a detour into a shady grotto and then pass the remains of a Roman aqueduct.

Start out at the CHATEAU in **Le Tholonet.** Walk west along the D17 for 250m/yds, then turn right on the **Chemin de la Paroisse.** Ignore tracks off to houses but, when you come to a knoll on the right, you will notice that it is riddled with paths. Take the wide path furthest to the left (*not waymarked*), at first climbing parallel with the lane. The path widens out, and you head east to the base of a rocky outcrop, through pines and holm oak.
After passing above the BACK OF THE CHATEAU (**15min**), the path curves to the left and drops. At a fork go either way — just head for the sound of rushing water below. After a short steep descent, you

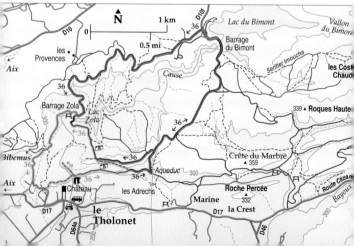

come to a narrow IRRIGATION DITCH: turn left on the path beside it (it's slightly overgrown at first, but then excellent). You come to a FORD SHADED BY PLANE TREES (**25min**), an unusual setting for a picnic. (If you are intrigued by off-beat places, continue ahead a short way past the ford, to where the stream threads through gorges, and some intrepid explorers have made a 'path' through the wilderness with logs and ferns.) From

Approaching Lac Zola

the ford return the way you came, past your descending path. Ford a shallow stream and walk ahead to a wide track. On your right now are the scant remains of a ROMAN AQUEDUCT, where a waterfall disgorges into a lovely pool. Follow the track (RED WAYMARKS) uphill through pine and oak, with white cliffs all around you. You come to two METAL POSTS (**1h**), where a faint path goes left towards a rock wall. Ignore this but, just beyond it, turn left on a good strong path (GREEN WAY-MARKS). *(The Alternative walks continue straight ahead here, along the track.)* There are paths all along here, so keep ahead (northwest) on the main path, weaving through limestone boulders. As you double back above your out-going route, you can see it below on the left, in a small valley swamped with pines. After 10 minutes you join the main track to the dam: bear left downhill. After just a couple of minutes there is a beautiful view of the jade-green lake from some rocks off to the right. The Croix de Provence rises on the right, challenging you to try Walk 35. When you reach **Lac Zola** (**1h25min**), cross the DAM. It was built in the mid-19th century by the father of Emile Zola (see page 56), and was the first arched dam in the world. The rock ledges here are good picnic spots. Take the metalled lane leading uphill from the dam, passing the old KEEPER'S HOUSE on the right (now run by the Office National des Forêts). Soon a wide track curves in front of you in a big U-bend (**1h45min**); this leads to Bibemus, where Cézanne used to paint. Don't curve uphill to Bibemus, go left downhill on the lane. Some 15 minutes later you pass the knoll at the start of the walk and continue back to the CHATEAU in **Le Tholonet** (**2h10min**).

TRAIN DES PIGNES

Departures: from Nice daily at about 6.40, 09.00, 12.40 and 17.00; from Digne at 07.00, 10.30, 14.00, 17.30. *Journey time 3h15min*. There are other departures from both ends of the line, but the trains do not cover the entire route: obtain the latest timetable at Nice or one of the stations (see **bold type** below). The operators (Chemins de Fer de Provence; see 'Public transport' on the touring map) also run a touristic steam train between Puget-Théniers and Annot.

Hints: The little train is very comfortable, with large padded seats and 'sightseeing-size' windows. Travelling south, sit on the left-hand side; travelling north, sit on the right. *Don't* make the mistake of sitting in the front row — the ticket collector monopolises the front windows! Take a map, to pin-point all the sights en route. The train stops for a good five minutes at Annot, where those 'in the know' alight to have a cup of coffee at the pleasant station restaurant.

No trip to the south of France is complete without a journey on the delightful Train des Pignes (named for the pine nuts the crew collected on the runs to stoke the steam engines). After the County of Nice was returned to France in 1860, there was great interest in linking the newly re-won Alps (see photo caption page 87) with the coast. Every valley wanted its own train. One of the surprisingly numerous projects to get off the drawing board, despite obstacles of terrain and financing, was the line built from Nice to Digne between 1890 and 1912 — spanning 150km via 16 viaducts, 17 bridges, and 25 tunnels, one of them 3km long! Some other railways built at this time, at enormous cost and effort, have not survived: the viaducts on the line to Barcelonnette are now drowned beneath the Lac de Serre-Ponçon; the Caramel Viaduct passed on Car tour 2 is the sad remains of the route from Menton to Sospel.

The train is not only worth taking for the sightseeing, but an extremely pleasant way to get to walks (Walks 25 and 26 lie en route). It's a 'friendly' train, too, and will stop to drop off or pick up walkers virtually anywhere along the run. At all the stations you should be able to find a pocket guide, *Randonnées Pédestres avec le Train des Pignes*. If you read French, it contains a wealth of ideas, *but* the walks vary enormously in interest and difficulty and *should not be attempted without the relevant large-scale IGN map!* Leaving Nice, the train moves like a tram through the city and into the suburbs. Soon it's hurtling along the wide basin of the *Var*. At **Colomars** look up left, above the industrial spread of modern-day Carros beside the Var, to *Carros-Village* and *Le Broc* perched on the hillside. At **St-Martin-du-Var**, the *Esteron Valley* comes in from the left. Beyond **Plan-du-Var**, don't miss the mouth of the *Vésubie Gorge*, seen through the Pont Durandy on the right. The perched village of *Bonson* rises on the left. Now you're in the *Defilé du Chaudan*, between the two carriageways of the N202, racing the motorists. Utelle cannot be seen above the olive terraces, but *do* look out right (just beyond a tunnel) for the towering walls of

Trains at Annot (top left), one of them prepared for a snowfall. Vauban's gate at Entrevaux (far left) and Puget-Théniers station. Above: near the Chambre du Roi (Walk 26, which begins and ends at Annot station).

the *Tinée Gorge,* backed by the *Mercantour.* Small farmholdings introduce **Toüet-sur-Var,** huddled below a rock cliff. Then the most magnificent of all the gorges opens up — the *Cians Gorge.* Look up to the rock blades behind **Puget-Théniers**: Alternative walk 25 scales those cliffs. A 5km-long stretch of orchards and planes lines the way from here to **Entrevaux,** the fairy-tale village shown on page 36.

Past the gap of the *Daluis Gorge,* watch for some high bluffs on the right: Walk 26 rounds a ledge almost at the very top. At **Annot** notice the houses built into boulders like those shown in the top right-hand photograph *(Grès d'Annot)* and the chaos of *grès* just as you leave, as well as the *robines* (see page 133). Now the train hurtles through the rolling fields

and orchards of the verdant *Vaïre Valley* to **Méailles**. A 3km-long tunnel precedes **Thorame-Haute-Gare**. Still the little train tears along, shrugging off the fact that it has already climbed 1000m from Nice! The gorgeous *Verdon Valley* is followed to **St-André**. You have a fine view of the church and the *Lac de Castillon* as you leave: watch for paragliders here. Following the *Asse de Moriez,* come to **Moriez**: just outside it there are interesting rock dikes. A 12th-century chapel rises on a hill outside **Barrême**, where a huge fir graces the station. Now the N85 *(Route Napoléon)* is just beside you on the right, and you skirt the *Forêt Domaniale des Trois Asses,* as you follow the Asse de Blieux via the *Clue de Chabrières* (on the left) to **Châteauredon**. From here the train curves north and crosses the wide *Bléone,* before coming into **Digne** (*i*❉**M**), below the Alpes de Haute-Provence. Out of the station, turn left to walk into the town (about 15 minutes).

131

GLOSSARY

Baume: cave, shelter beneath rock
Belvédère: elevated viewpoint
Bergerie: shelter for animals (and sometimes shepherds)
Buvette: snack bar
CAF: Club Alpin Français
Calanque: rocky inlet
Castelas, castellas, castellaras: old ruined castle; see Walk 18.
Chasse privée: private hunting ground
Cime: summit, peak, top
Cirque: a valley ending in a deep rounded 'amphitheatre' of rock (photographs pages 8-9, 86-87, 92)
Clos: enclosed parcel of cultivated land
Clue: narrow gorge or rift, cut by a watercourse perpendicularly to a chain of mountains; see Car tours 6 and 7 and photograph below.
Col: pass
Dégustation: wine-tasting
Dike: basaltic magma injected into a fissure in rocks, sometimes weathered into a wall-like form
Dolomitic rock: rock composed of soluble calcium and less soluble magnesium. The calcium erodes more quickly under the action of rainwater and streams, giving rise to weird formations, for which the French have a very apt name (*ruiniform*).
Domaine: property (vineyard)
Garrigue, Maquis: terrain resulting from the degradation of the Mediterranean forest (through fires or grazing), differentiated by the nature of their soil and characteristic flora. The *garrigue* is an open limestone wasteland on non-acidic soil, with small pockets of vegetation. Typical plants include Aleppo pines, kermes oak, holm oak, box, thistles, gorse, rough grass and wild aromatic plants like lavender, thyme and rosemary. The *maquis* is a dense covering of evergreen plants growing on acidic soil, usually with small hairy or leathery leaves to help withstand the dry conditions. Flora include trees like cork and holm oaks, junipers, box, strawberry trees and myrtle, as well as smaller bushes like rosemary, jerusalem sage, broom, heather, and *Cistus.* Larger trees like chestnuts and maritime pines may also be present.
Gouffre: gulf, abyss
GR (Grande Randonnée): long-distance footpath, waymarked with red and white paint flashes; see page 62.
Grès: sand- or gritstone, eroded into strange shapes. A chaos of gigantic sandstone rocks and arches is the most prominent feature of the landscape around Annot; photographs pages 110, 131 (Walk 26).
Grotte: cave
Maquis: see Garrigue
Maquis, The: French Resistance during World War II
Mas: country house, usually applied to a farm
Massif: mountain mass with several peaks
Oppidum: defensive position of dry-stone walls at vantage points. The

Left: strawberry tree (top) and the Clue de St-Auban (Car tour 7)

The Roche Taillée ('cut rock'; Walk 19) was hewn out by the Romans to accommodate a watercourse.

Ligurians built the first *oppida*. See Walk 18.

PR (Petite Randonnée): local way-marked walk, fairly short, often circular; see page 62.

Porphyry rock: hard rock in which crystals of one or more minerals are deposited; the colour depends on the metallic content. Red porphyry rock characterises the Esterel (Car tour 1 and Walks 5-7), but you will also find small examples of blue or green porphyry rock.

Rive droite, rive gauche: right bank, left bank of a river. (The banks of a river are defined *from* the source.)

Robines (roubines): limey-clay slopes prone to erosion. They form steep and slippery gulleys — difficult walking terrain. Prevalent in Haute-Provence, they are the most obvious feature of the landscape around St-André (Car tour 5); photographs pages 113 and right.

Roche, Rocher: rock

Route Napoléon: The N85, opened in 1932. See Car tour 4 and photographs on page 101 and the cover.

Ruiniform: a word the French use to describe a chaos of dolomitic rock, which has eroded into the shape of ruins. They may look like a building or even a whole town, or sometimes a ruined sculpture. The Cadières de Brandis, shown on page 7, are an example of *ruiniform* dolomitic rock.

Sentier (botanique): footpath. (A *sentier botanique* is usually accompanied by information panels describing the botany and geology of a specific area; there is a particularly interesting *sentier botanique* at the Lac d'Allos, Walk 23.)

Table d'orientation: panoramic viewpoint, usually with a circular stone 'table' marked with the points of the compass and pin-pointing the location of towns, mountains, etc.

Transhumance: periodic migration of sheep, in order to graze on the high mountains in summer and return to the lower slopes in the autumn. This movement of flocks has been carried out by lorry in modern times, but in the last few years some shepherds have returned to the ancient practice of making the journey with their flocks on foot.

Via: road. By 100BC Rome held much of the land between the Alps and the Pyrenees. Their most important highways were the *Via Agrippa* via Orange and Avignon to Arles, the *Via Aurelia* via Nice, Fréjus, Aix and Nimes to Arles and then Spain (today the N7 follows much the same route), and the *Via Domitia* via Sisteron, Apt and Pont Julien south to the *Via Aurelia*.

Right: robines *near the Crête d'Aurafort (Alternative walk 25)*

● Index

Geographical names comprise the only entries in this Index; for non-geographical names, see Contents, page 3. A page number in *italic type* indicates a map; a page number in **bold type** indicates a photograph. Both of these may be in addition to a text reference on the same page.